Reflections of Seattle's Chinese Americans:
The First 100 Years

Edited by Ron Chew
& Cassie Chinn

Wing Luke Asian Museum, Seattle

Note on Chinese Language
The first Chinese immigrants to Seattle came from the small district of Toisan in Southeast China. They spoke Toisanese, which is similar to Cantonese, but very different from Mandarin, the national language of China. Chinese words and places in this book have been anglicized according to Cantonese and Toisanese - the way these immigrants would have learned them in school and at home.

Cover and publication: Abe Wong

Wing Luke Asian Museum
407 Seventh Avenue South
Seattle, Washington 98104

Copyright © 2003 by the Wing Luke Asian Museum
Printed in the United States of America

All rights reserved. No part of this publication may be reproduced or transmitted in any form or by any means, electronic or mechanical, including photocopy, recording, or any information storage or retrieval system, without permission in writing from the publisher.

ISBN 0-9746741-0-9 (paperback)

The paper used in this publication meets the minimum requirements of American National Standard for Information Sciences, Permanence of Paper of Printed Library Materials, ANSI Z39.48-1984.

Editors' Note

This second edition publication, which began as a modest Chinese American oral history project over 13 years ago, has passed through countless hands along the way as it grew into this book. Although there is a more complete list of acknowledgments in the back, there are some honorable mentions that belong here, front and center.

First, we would like to thank our prime sponsor, the Tuai family, for generously stepping forward with a substantial contribution to cover a large portion of the production costs. Second, we would like to acknowledge The Boeing Company for providing in-kind printing support. Third, we thank Bon-Macy*s for a major financial contribution.

For this second edition of *Reflections of Seattle's Chinese Americans*, we would like to highlight the following key individuals: Doug Chin, for writing the essay on Chinese American history; John D. Pai and Dean Wong, for portrait photography; Abe Wong, for publication design; Vivian Chan, for publication supervision; Melissa Szeto Matsuda, for research and additional interviews; Jeni Kay Fung and Donnie Chin, for on-going advice and consultation; Zuo-lie Deng and Reverend Paul Szeto, for Chinese calligraphy; Elizabeth Umbanhowar, for proofreading; and Bob Fisher, for historic photo selection.

We would like to thank the Wing Luke Asian Museum, both its board and staff, for unwavering support for this project, which came under the wing of the institution when we joined the Museum as staff members in the early 1990s. The full transcripts of the interviews, excerpted for this book, are now housed in the permanent archive of the Museum.

Finally, we offer our deepest gratitude to the dozens of Chinese American elders who generously shared their memories with us as we began to piece together an untold past that we came to understand and embrace as our own. To them and their families, we dedicate this book.

Ron Chew and Cassie Chinn
Co-Editors

Table of Contents

Editors' Note..........................2
A Message from the
　Tuai Family........................4
A Message from
　The Boeing Company..........4
A Message from
　Bon-Macy*s........................4
Preface: First Edition...............5
Preface: Second Edition..........6

Part I: Portraits

Florence Chin Eng................8
Hing W. Chinn....................10
Harry Wong........................12
Ruby Au Chinn....................14
Patricia Au Kan...................16
Ken Louie...........................18
Walter Chinn......................20
Roy Chu.............................22
Tek Wong...........................23
James Wong.......................24
Henry Louie.......................26
Fannie Eng Lung.................28
Violette Chan.....................29
Louise Yook.......................30
Nellie Chinn Woo................31
James Mar.........................32
Loy Hugh Locke.................34
Bill Kay..............................36
Priscilla Chong Jue.............38
Anne Chinn Wing...............40
Henry H. Woo....................42
Helen Woo Locke...............44
Clifton Goon......................45
Marjorie L. Lee...................46
Harriett Wu........................48
Myra Mar Chin...................49
Raymond Chinn..................50
Bill L. Chin.........................52
Mary Luke Woo..................54
Josephine Chinn Woo..........56
Rose Chinn Wong...............58
Paul Louie.........................60
Jeni Dong Mar....................62
James Louie......................64
William Eng......................66
Winnie Tuai......................68
Jessie Edwards..................69
Wallace "Pudge" Eng..........70
Henry Chin.......................72
Andrew Chinn...................73
Henry Kay Lock.................74
Henry Hing.......................76
Nancy Jang.......................78
Bruce Dong.......................80
Guay Lee..........................82
Ben Woo...........................84
Hing Y. Chinn....................86
Melvin Woo......................88
Wilma C. Woo...................89
Sam Yee............................90
Gregory H. Chew...............92
Alfred C. Mar....................94
Mary Woo.........................96
Chong Wing Mar...............98
Lohman Jang....................99
May G. Woo....................100
Mary Doung Chinn..........101
Jeni Kay Fung..................102
David H. Woo..................104
James Locke....................106
Bill Lee............................108
Eugene Ko......................110
Richard Lew Kay.............112
Hen Sen Chin..................114
Frank L. Chong................116
Hong Y. Chin...................118
Dorothy Chun..................120
Wai Eng..........................122
Daniel Hong Lew.............124
Sen Poy Chew.................126
Gee Min Lee...................128
Lee Hong "Smiley" Young.129
Yu Sung Chin..................130
Gim Chin........................131
Gam Har Chew................132
Fung Sinn Wong..............134
Puey King Wong.............135
Toy Kay..........................136
Gertrude Jue...................137
Tsee Watt Mark...............138
Ruth Mar........................139
George Ham...................140
Frances Chin Ho.............142
Vincent Y. Dong.............144
Art Louie.......................146
Keye Luke......................148
Helen Eng Kay...............150
Ruby Chow....................152
Art B. Lum....................154
Lawrence P. Chinn.........156
Eddie Moy....................158
Henry Louie..................160
Dan Mar.......................161
Steven Luke..................162
Homer Wong.................164
James Yee.....................166
George K. Yee...............167
Warren Chan.................168
Liem Eng Tuai..............170
Calvin Fung..................172
Allan Fay Wong............173
Ruth Jung Chinn...........174

Part II: A History of Seattle's Chinese Americans

The First Arrivals................176
The Anti-Chinese
　Movement........................180
Establishing a Permanent
　Settlement......................182
From Sojourners to
　Immigrants....................186
Growth of the
　Community....................191
Bibliography....................196
Index of Individuals in
　Alphabetical Order with
　Listing of Immediate Family
　Relationships within the
　Book, and Interview and
　Photograph Credits..........197
Acknowledgments............201

A Message from the Tuai Family

Our family's strong interest in preserving the stories of Seattle's Chinese American history is in large part because we have been here a long time – we're "Longtime Washington," you might say. Our mother, Winnie Joyce Tuai, neé Eng, was born and raised in what was then called Seattle's Chinatown. Our father, Liem Eng Tuai, was born in Port Townsend and grew up, for the most part, in Bremerton. The three of us, their sons, were all born and raised in Seattle.

The stories of our parents, relatives and other Chinese Americans in Seattle are quickly disappearing. It is important to know those who came before us and to understand their accomplishments, sacrifices and aspirations. We need to realize that our place in society did not just happen; it was the result of many battles, large and small.

We hear of the first Chinese American to win an Olympic medal, the first to be Governor, the first to serve on the Seattle City Council and the first to run for Mayor of Seattle. Today, such achievements are increasingly common and are no longer necessarily described with statements such as "the first Chinese American" or "the first Asian American." This book not only tells the stories of those "first" people who were at the vanguard of reforms, changes and leadership, but also the stories of those who struggled to simply make ends meet after coming to America.

As part of our parents' legacy, we're proud to be able to support this second edition of *Reflections of Seattle's Chinese Americans: The First 100 Years*. Our parents would be happy to know we have helped preserve the stories of our community for their grandchildren and future generations. This book is a tribute to all of our parents, grandparents and great grandparents.

Walter, Gregory and David Tuai

A Message from The Boeing Company

The Boeing Company is pleased to support the new edition of *Reflections of Seattle's Chinese Americans: The First 100 Years*, and is honored to join you in celebrating the rich heritage of this important and vibrant Seattle community. The Puget Sound area is home to thousands of Boeing employees. We love this area and cherish its cultural diversity. We congratulate you and applaud this fine effort, and are confident "Reflections" will be not only a tribute to our friends in the Chinese American community and to their many contributions, but also a thoughtful and poignant reminder that the true quality of a city can be measured by the appreciation and respect we have for each other.

We wish you well, and hope the next 100 years brings an equally rich mix of memories, progress and admiration.

A Message from Bon-Macy*s

We, at Bon-Macy*s, would like to offer our heartfelt support and best wishes for your new edition of *Reflections of Seattle's Chinese Americans: The First 100 Years*. Chinese Americans have been – and will continue to be – a cultural force within Seattle's diverse community. Their economic, artistic, social and religious contributions have been a source of pride and inspiration for all people. Your book gives this rich history the compelling narration it so rightfully deserves.

We're proud to have sponsored such a worthwhile endeavor as *Reflections of Seattle's Chinese Americans*. Accept our congratulations and our hope that the next 100 years will be just as eventful.

Preface: First Edition

Ask Seattleites what they know of Chinese American history. Most respondents would be at a loss to speak. At best, some might mention that the Chinese built the railroads, drawing from a stock image of men with straw hats, bent over picks and shovels, toiling industriously. Seattleites would be hard pressed, however, to describe much more.

But it was not simply through the building of the railroads that the Chinese left their imprint on history. The railroads were one episode in a larger saga, which stretches up through present day.

Pacific Rim trade, for example, is not a novel venture; it was a way of life for the first Chinese American pioneers. In 1868, Chin Chun Hock founded the Wa Chong Company, a famous Chinese American merchandise house, which continued well into the 20th century. Chin, the first Chinese settler in Seattle, arrived in 1860, nine years before Seattle was incorporated as a city.

The Chinese worked in the sawmills and the coal mines. They cleared land and graded the streets. They dug the first canal connecting Lake Union with Lake Washington. They planted, harvested and peddled vegetables. They worked as net fishermen in Elliott Bay. They worked in restaurants, laundries, dry goods stores and other businesses throughout the city. In later years, they nudged their way into the mainstream: becoming engineers, insurance salesmen, architects, lawyers, teachers, doctors and politicians.

The early Chinese arrivals called themselves *Gim San hok*, guests of Gold Mountain or the United States. But before long, they began to see America not simply as a workplace, but also as a permanent home. Even in 1886, at the height of the anti-Chinese fervor, when white rioters dragged the Chinese from their Seattle homes and forced most of them out of town on steamers, a few merchants, laundry men and servants remained. They preserved an unbroken Chinese American presence. And when the Great Seattle Fire of 1889 leveled the city's business district, other Chinese workers returned to help rebuild.

It is unfortunate that Seattleites do not know this deep history, even those who are descendants of the early Chinese pioneers, bearing direct claim to this past. In many Chinese families, the older people never told the stories, and the children never bothered to ask. Most of our stories have been swallowed up in the silence between generations, in the chasm between youthful disinterest and old world privacy. Those who came here under paper identities during the long period of the Chinese Exclusion Act hid many of the stories from their children, who are now grown and have children of their own yearning for these clues to their family roots.

This book is an attempt to retrieve the stories. It contains portraits of 71 elders in Seattle's Chinese American community, who share, for the first time, their personal memories, both sweet and bitter. They were interviewed for the Chinese Oral History Project of Seattle, a community-wide undertaking which pooled the efforts of over 30 Chinese Americans – including students, social workers, community journalists and long-time Seattle residents. From 1990 through 1994, project members entered Chinatown stores, family associations, homes, community centers and workplaces to find, interview and photograph individuals. Later, they spent innumerable hours transcribing the tape-recorded conversations, checking information, gathering documents and identifying old photos.

In the interviews, pieces of which are presented here, the community elders take us back in time. They tell about the insular world of their childhood – the steamship voyage to America, interrogation in the immigration station, and the early days of Chinatown. They recall their passage into adulthood – starting school, adopting American identities, enduring the first harsh stabs of racial discrimination, working in the restaurants and salmon canneries, vying to gain independence from parents. They remember the era of World War II – when they served overseas, and entered jobs at the Boeing Company, and found access to work arenas outside Chinatown. They tell about their jobs, friends, families and social endeavors. In retirement, they describe their continuing dreams, now in the hands of the children they bore and the community they fostered.

Sixty-three interviews conducted in English are presented here through the actual words of the interview subjects, with only slight editing for grammar. Eight other subjects, who chose to speak in Toisanese, the language of most Chinese immigrants to Seattle prior to the 1960s, are presented through approximations of their words and thoughts.

The stories are supplemented by an original historical essay on Seattle's Chinese American community, written by Doug Chin, presented as Part II of this book. In 1973, Chin and his brother, Art, authored the first book on Chinese Americans in Seattle, *Uphill: The Settlement and Diffusion of the Chinese in Seattle, Washington*. Doug Chin created this new essay by combining his previous research with bountiful new sources of historical detail gathered from this oral history project.

Chin's historical text provides a window for understanding the struggles and achievements of Chinese Americans, a homogeneous and tight-knit community, during the period from 1860 to the 1960s. During this first 100 years, most Chinese Americans traced their origins to Kwangtung Province in Southeast China, to modest peasant villages in Toisan and other nearby districts. This was a contained Chinese American community: mostly men, few women and few families, encircled by prejudice and intolerance.

In the 1960s, the ground shifted and the tightly checked community began to overflow traditional boundaries. A dramatic change in U.S. immigration law, coupled with the Civil Rights Movement, allowed Chinese to come in greater numbers and presented bright new opportunities for the generation emerging. Immigrants poured in from many parts of China, Taiwan, Hong Kong, Vietnam and other countries in Southeast Asia. Those coming of age in America flocked to colleges and universities. Chinese Americans began settling in suburban areas such as Bellevue and Mercer Island, tasting the rewards of hard-won professional careers.

Chinatown changed, too. Not so long ago, the voices of the Toisan immigrants and their children rang through the streets of Chinatown, spilling from shops along King Street, from smoky restaurant kitchens that opened out onto back alleys, from the balconies and storefronts of tongs and family associations, from empty lots converted into play fields by children. New voices now fill the air as Chinatown passes gradually into the hands of a generation armed with more education, new skills and greater mobility.

We should not forget those who came before. These pioneers squeezed much out of the limited openings given them, gave back more than they took, built, stone by stone, the institutions of the Chinese community, and endured financial hardships and racial affronts so that they could provide for their families and children. From their stories, shared here, we honor this legacy and reclaim, at long last, our Chinese American history.

Ron Chew
July, 1994

Preface: Second Edition

Nearly a decade has come and gone since the publication of *Reflections of Seattle's Chinese Americans: The First 100 Years*. To our surprise, this modest local publication sold out within a year of its publication. This happy outcome was abetted by the relatively small run – we only printed 2,200 copies – and by an eager readership – people loved the unpretentious, heartfelt stories and portraits in the collection.

For several reasons, the second edition of what has come to be known simply as "Reflections" has been slow in making its way to publication, despite a continuing loud clamor for the book. "When are you going to reprint the book?" Over the years, this straightforward directive came to us – via the Wing Luke Asian Museum – almost weekly, from the lips of local family members whose loved ones were featured in the publication and from those with a special interest in Chinese American history. It was never a question of *whether* we were going to reprint it – it was always a question of *when*.

Here's why it took so long for this second delivery. First, we needed time to make corrections to the text and re-shoot portrait pictures. Second, many more oral histories – including those of war-brides and garment workers and others thinly represented in the first edition – flowed into our hands in the glowing aftermath of the book's publication. It was as if someone suddenly pulled open a jammed closet door and a hidden trove of stories came tumbling free. At the Museum, we needed time to interview, transcribe, translate, fact-check, edit and assemble these new finds. Lastly, we needed to raise a pile of money to support the printing costs.

At the core of this book are carefully selected excerpts from taped interviews with the men and women of the World War II generation. Their little stories are clear, strong and full of unrestrained pride. They spent most of their years in a simpler, harsher era, when a full stomach and a complete education were promised to no one, when hard work and sacrifice overrode personal freedom, when "providing" for the family was cherished as a crown achievement. In these stories, we see the earthy texture of a Chinatown that has now passed into folklore and the gradual emergence of a modern Chinese American perspective, born out of a more open and prosperous society.

"Reflections" has now bulked up to 102 featured interviews and portraits for this second edition, compared with 71 in the first edition. Of the original 71 subjects, 27 have passed away. Of the additional

31 more recent interview subjects in this second edition, 11 of them have also died, too. Says Jimmy Mar, funeral director for the Chinese community, whose story is featured here, "They're all passing away now. Some weeks, I handle two or three funerals. It's very sad. I think within 10 years, most of the Chinese family associations will be gone, too." Uncle Jimmy still works out of Yick Fung & Company, a dimly-lit pioneer store on South King Street, the main street along Chinatown. Uncle Jimmy is a rarity, too; most of his contemporaries are already gone.

Earlier this year, I attended a funeral service for an old-timer I knew as Uncle Ming – *Ming bok*. For the record, his American name was Yee Young Pung. He was a short, stocky man whose black-framed glasses, round head and large forehead gave him an owl-like appearance. He spoke little, and had a stoic, but bright demeanor. He was a man of the restaurant – *key hoy ga* – a waiter. He worked for decades alongside my father at the old Hong Kong Restaurant, a popular Chinatown establishment, which, though closed for nearly two decades now, still boasts a large vertical neon sign on its front façade, a reminder of what once was. *Ming bok* was among the last of the old-timers who spent a lifetime as a Chinatown waiter, working, during most of his career, for a dollar an hour or less, without vacation, sick leave and pension – cheated, as those of his generation were, of the benefits of the modern workplace.

Ming bok was born in 1912 in China and came to New York City in 1923. His first job was peeling potatoes in a restaurant. For 20 months, he peeled potatoes. Ten to 11 hours a day, seven days a week. He didn't receive any pay, but he ate free. During my growing up years, through the '50s, '60s and '70s, he had already settled into a six-day-a-week work ritual at the Hong Kong Restaurant. He was the first one to arrive at the restaurant and the last one to leave. He and my father were the two most popular waiters at the restaurant; I knew because, as a busboy clearing tables, I gathered their tips for them, and their takes were invariably the heftiest of all the waiters. They knew how to serve. Regular customers would ask for my dad or *Ming bok* when they came to the restaurant.

The rain was pouring heavily when I attended the Saturday morning funeral service for Uncle Ming at the chapel of the funeral home on Queen Anne Hill. I was surprised that there were no more than 10 individuals, mostly relatives, scattered throughout the pews. Maybe the rain kept some folks away. Uncle Ming had also outlived most of his co-workers; and the many families he once served had either forgotten him or didn't know that he had died.

The minister's sermon for *Ming bok* was delivered with the obligatory religious phrases to ease the intense sorrow of his widow and family and to close the book on his life. But I was surprised at the sparseness of detail about Uncle Ming's life. Who was this man? Ninety years of life on earth reduced to a few sentences of text. The elusive particulars of Uncle Ming's life – like those of so many Chinese men who came to America during the period of the Chinese Exclusion Act – remained whispered or unspoken, carried finally to the grave like a set of sealed tomes.

In the past decade, so many individuals like Uncle Ming – the adults of my childhood, the old-timers of my adulthood, the men and women of the Depression and World War II, heralded by Tom Brokaw as "The Greatest Generation" – have passed into old age and death. The shift is now nearly complete. What we share here in this book are a collection of personal episodes from their lives, stories that appease our curiosity, inspire the heart and reduce the mystery of who we are and how we came to be. These stories, retrieved from the dustbin of time, allow our children to someday walk confidently in their tall shadows.

Ron Chew
November, 2003

Florence Chin Eng worked continuously at the Wa Sang Company, a grocery store in Chinatown, from 1928, when her father opened the business, until the store closed in 1997. The New Eagle Café, a coffee shop, had previously occupied the space.

Florence Chin Eng

Born 1909, Hoy Jew Village, Toisan District, Kwangtung Province, China
Died February, 2001, Seattle, Washington

My grandfather was here in the 1880s. Then my father came in 1909 on a student visa. My father couldn't afford to go to regular school in those days. He worked in the lumber camps and later moved over to Portland and worked in a restaurant called the Cat in a Fiddle. I came over with my mother in 1923.

My father inherited my grandfather's business, and as a merchant, you can bring in your family. That's the reason I can come. I came by boat. Twenty-one days on the ocean. We rode third class. I wanted to go up to the deck and look around and see what I can find. All I can see is just fog and couldn't see not too far, not even a bird. Before we left home, my mother said, "When you see anything on the ocean, don't ask me about it." She was superstitious. I saw sea lions as big as elephants, and then I wouldn't dare to ask my mother anything. I just look at it.

There were some friends who were working in the ship. They are what we call our cousins – *hung thling, nah sook, bak*. They were underneath the first class. Every day, I took a little time and walked over to those places, and they gave me cakes and apples. Every day, I go there and come back to eat and come back down to sleep.

One day, it was kind of snowy, and the deck is very slippery. I had my slippers on and I fell. It's a good thing that I hang onto the railing. After that, I'm too scared to go up until we get to Victoria. Then we made a stop in Vancouver and then over to Seattle where the ship stopped.

I was locked for two weeks in immigration – not this one – the old one, down pretty close to the Pike Place Market. Sometime when you see your father down there, he would come to look at you through the window – but no talking. The women, they put them in a separate room and then the men in a separate floor. They watch you just like a hawk. They check your human waste, urine and everything.

I went to the foreign class with people who came in from all over – Europe, China or Japan. It used to be in Pacific School. I stayed there for about a year and a half and then later on, I was assigned to the Bailey Gatzert at the fifth grade. After sixth grade, I went back to Pacific. I only completed the seventh grade. I didn't have a chance to go to eighth. Because all my brothers and sisters were all little, my father was the only one that come out to work. So I came out here to work with my father. I want to go to school some more, and my father didn't even make me, but I offered.

During the Depression, my father started opening the restaurants. That was in 1933. He opened one up at Eighth and Pike called the Wa Sang Café. Then he opened the Shanghai over in Bremerton the same year, and in 1938, he opened the restaurant, Lun Ting, at the University District, right next to the bookstore. My father was killed in a car accident in 1940. Then that's the time that's pretty rough. After my father died, people in town said, "Give those guys six months. Everything will be gone with the wind." I couldn't stand what people say. I talked to my mom, "Dad paid everything. He didn't owe anybody. His business is all paid up. It's clear. I try to run it." I didn't have any skills. I'm not an educated person. I got muscle, and thank God, I didn't get sick at all. The way I look at it, someday when the children grow up, they stay together, at least we have a family. But if I can't do it, my dad knows I tried. One thing is I have to stick with my family.

Hing W. Chinn

Born June 1, 1930, Bo Yin Fong Village, Toisan District, Kwangtung Province, China

You had to go through immigration regardless. People stay there for a few months, some of them years. You stay there less than a month, you are lucky. I think I stayed a couple or three weeks. They ask all kind of questions, match with your dad's questioning. See if the answers match or not. Make sure you're a real son.

It's just like a jail house. Bunk beds, metal bars. Except in a jail house you have two people to a room. Here, you have 20 or 30 people in a room. At lunchtime or dinnertime, they open the middle gate and they let you out. You line up for lunch and sit down in this cafeteria at these benches and tables.

They ask silly questions. If I remember, those questions related to your house. They ask you how many chairs you got in the house. Where do you keep your rice barrel, the *mai gong*? How many windows in your house? How many kitchen windows? Which way do they face? Is your house the third one in a row from the road? How many trips did your father go back and forth from China?

You have to prove you are the real McCoy. A lot of people are real sons, but they can't get out because the answers doesn't match. At that time, you are guilty until you are proven you're not. Before we came over, we memorized all those questions. Your parents always tell you, you have to memorize. If you don't answer correctly, they kick you back.

When the Chinese first came over, they worked 12 to 16 hour days. Now, the younger generation doesn't work like that anymore. Eight hour day, and that's it. I think that's why you see a lot of those small grocery stores by new immigrants. They work hard like our forefathers.

I think the family associations all need new blood, the younger people to get involved more. That's the problem. Most of the older people are dying out. Before, the older people – the people who used to hang around Chinatown – they really used to give their time. If the association needs money, everybody donates. A lot of people are busy nowadays. You try to go ask for donations, it's kind of hard. It's not like it used to be.

The Oak Tin Association has a board. When I was on the board, they helped solve problems like cheating. If restaurant partnerships have disagreements, they are brought to the board, and they kind of solved it, and they obeyed. Now, everybody goes to the attorneys and gets legal advice.

All of my kids are born here. We took them back to the village. At first, they asked what kind of toilet they have there. It kind of scared them. We stayed at the hotel. It's not bad. We never stayed in the village. We stayed in town. I think they enjoyed it. See how different cultures live so they will appreciate the United States more.

At the age of nine, Hing Chinn came to Seattle to join his father, a bookkeeper for the Tuck Shing Company. He grew up in Chinatown. Later, as president of the Gee How Oak Tin Family Association, he spearheaded the successful renovation of his association's building in Chinatown in 1990.

陳慰庭

Harry Wong is best remembered for working at Seattle's Trader Vic's Restaurant in the Westin Hotel. Through his position at the restaurant, he traveled to other Trader Vic's Restaurants throughout the world and met many famous politicians and actors.

Harry Wong

Born January 10, 1923, Chai Yuen Village, Toisan District, Kwangtung Province, China
Died March 15, 2002, Seattle, Washington

My grandfather, my father was over here, and my grandmother was over here, too. My grandfather was an herbalist, and he does all the contracting work for the canneries in Alaska, supplies manpower. It is a business. He does a lot of things. He's like go-between, between the early Chinese community and the outside. Like you need a lawyer, you go to him. You need a doctor. They'll do all that stuff. He contract for the cannery, and he contract for the immigration station. He has the contract for feeding those people. He hired the people to cook the food in the station and serve them.

We were in a large village, about 100 houses. We have our own school until sixth grade. My childhood, we have a pretty easy life. We considered one of the better off people. I had never seen my grandfather in China, but my father come back every three years to China, just to visit for about eight, nine months, and then he'd come back to America. I was 13 when I came over. All the younger boys are looking forward to come over here, or go somewhere. If you stay in the village, you could either be a farmer or work in the store, which is very hard to get a job for, so you end up with just being a farmer. You can't get jobs for anything else.

We were on the President Line steamship, President McKinley. It took 22 days. Compare what you left in China, it's very comfortable. I waited four days in immigration, then I come up for question. You just sit there and wait. You just in a big room with all the people. They had bars in it and a lock. The room is like a dormitory. You get like 40, 50 people in there, and when time to eat, they'll open the gate and march you down to the dining hall and you eat there. Then after that, they bring you back and lock up again.

They pretty thorough and asked everything. Kind of trick questions and a lot of those questions they asked is not on the thing you prepared for. What's the location of the drinking well and what's in between and how do you go to town? Which way you go? You have to remember the date of birthdays and things like that. I could tell I didn't make any mistakes.

My whole family came to America. My mother was the only one never been over here. I was told that we had so much land in China so someone have to stay behind to look at. In those times, that was the way of life. The men come over here, make a living, and the wife stay back. The last time my father went back was to bring me over. Not long after that, he passed away. My mother gone through a tough life once the Communist took over because we consider a big landowner. They watch pretty close. She can't go anywhere. She can't leave the village. Some people go out of Hong Kong and eventually come over here, but she can't do that.

Ruby Au Chinn

Born October 5, 1915, Seattle, Washington
Died May 28, 1998, Seattle, Washington

My mother never saw my father until after she married him. They never talked together. It was all arranged by matchmakers with consent from the two families. My father was in Seattle. They were married with a rooster filling in.

The bride travels in a rickshaw to the family. They used a rooster to represent the groom. Someone holds the rooster, they bow before the rickshaw. The curtain is lifted and the bride goes into the groom's house. That bound them for life – until death do us part. As soon as everything was in order, she went to meet him in Washington.

That was fairly common in those times. With the Chinese, they go through their own rituals and they say their own vows. The Chinese believe that if two people want to make a vow, you go outside and keep your eyes on the heavens and you would say something like, "Before God we swear," and that would be it. That was years ago – the old Chinese customs. In a way, it's wonderful that people could keep their words just on a vow to one another, or go through some ritual, and having gone through that with another person, that's it. It's for life.

Altogether they had six children, two boys and four girls. We were all born in Washington, except the youngest girl who was born in Hong Kong. In 1920, we went back to Hong Kong. My mother had asthma so bad that the doctors said they could not guarantee her life if she stayed. My father stayed to send money back to support the family. He was able to send very little.

My father was the head of a tong. The tongs were like a labor union. Anyone could join if they paid dues. They were to protect you if anyone took advantage of you. Another tong was out to get him during the tong war. He was sick with influenza. He didn't dare go out to see the doctor. That's why, in about 1926, he went back to China. His tong brothers bought him a passage back on the steamer, gave him 200 American dollars, and because they knew he had a family back in China, put him on the boat. That's why you belonged to these tongs. They looked out for each other.

When my father went back, he was very sick. He wouldn't let anyone but his brother, an herbalist – doctor of Chinese medicine – treat him. He said, "I'm going to let my brother treat me until I die." He lived eight months. When he died, we didn't even have the money to bury him. My mother had to turn over some deeds on some rice fields in the village to get the money to bury him.

My mother told me after my father died that there would be no money for my education, and that if there was any money, it would go to the boys. So she asked me, "Would you like to go to Gold Mountain – *Gim San*?" I wasn't even 12 at the time. At that age, wouldn't you want to go somewhere? So I came over here where education is free and you don't have to pay.

It was sad. In those days, they would allow a merchant's wife to come over, but they would not allow a citizen's wife from overseas to come over. Some would try to bring their wife back over. Many would not because it was so difficult.

They would lock the wives up in immigration for months. You'd have to go through many sessions of questions to see if you were what you said. If they didn't believe you, they would send you back. They would just say, "This is not the truth." Some would commit suicide down there.

For over 70 years, Ruby Au Chinn was active in the Chinese Baptist Church, the sole religious institution in the Chinese community for many years. From 1958 to 1962, she taught English to women who recently emigrated from China. Classes were held in the mornings, five days a week.

Patricia Au Kan married George Kan in 1931. She met him while working in a salmon cannery in Ketchikan, Alaska.

簡區雪清

Patricia Au Kan

Born December 22, 1910, Ellensburg, Washington

My parents were merchants. We lived in a little downbeaten house next to the Chinese Baptist Church on Washington Street. There was no bathtub. You had a tin tub and heated water on the stove. When I was nine, the whole family returned to China because of my mother's health. She had asthma. The doctors said she would not get well if she stayed. If she would get away from here, she would be all right. Which was true – the minute she went to Hong Kong, she didn't have any asthma and she could eat anything. When she was here, she couldn't eat bean sprouts, she sat up all night with asthma. But when we went back to Hong Kong, she never had it.

We went back for seven years. In China, it was a little better. We had more to eat, better food, and relatives back there. We didn't have anybody here. I went to an English school in Hong Kong for a little while. I could speak English a little bit. School there was just like any other school. We learned in Chinese characters. When I started middle school, I came back to Seattle. I was not homesick for America. I had to come back to look for something to do. My mother thought that I would have better opportunities over here to work and maybe help the family. I liked eating bread better than rice.

We all came back at separate times. My sister Ruby came back first in July without her family. She went to New York City. Somebody took her in. She was 12 years old. I was 17 when I came back here to look for a living. I missed my family, but it couldn't be helped. My parents taught me how to take care of myself. I worked for Mar Dong. I was a telephone operator for the Mar Hotel. That was my first job. Then I went to the canneries with my cousin. He was the foreman of a fish cannery in Ketchikan, and we went there three years. Then I worked for a Chinese import-export shop.

I met my husband, George, in the cannery. That was in 1930. He was four years older than me. I liked him and I was living alone. He taught me to play tennis in Alaska. We got married in 1931. We went to the Justice of the Peace. I had a printed navy blue dress. During the Depression, he was a cabdriver to start with. That's all he could get. I took in sewing. I sewed sweaters at home. We lived on 24th and Charles for a while. Then we moved to an apartment on 14th. We got by. We were never rich. When the Second World War came on, someone let George buy their dry cleaning shop down on Stewart Street. It was owned by a Chinese man who was drafted. My husband and I ran it. We made a living out of it. Then we sold that and went up to 23rd and Jackson and opened another one. We called it Kan's Cleaners.

The happiest time of my life was when my son Kingsley came back from Vietnam. All my kids were in the military: Air Force, Navy and Army. Darryl went when he was 17. He went to the Navy. Stanton went to the Korean War. Kingsley went to Vietnam. And Cynthia went overseas, too. They volunteered. We didn't want them to go, but they had to go.

Ken Louie spent his early childhood in China. He came back to Seattle and completed public school. After graduating from the University of Washington, he joined his brother, Henry, in working full-time at their grandfather's business, the Tsue Chong Company, a noodle and fortune cookie factory in Chinatown.

Ken Louie

Born April 16, 1927, New York, New York
Died November 13, 2001, Seattle, Washington

We went back to China to get a little Chinese education about the time that the Depression was coming on. American money's worth more in China, so my dad stayed over here and worked as a waiter, cook, whatever he could do to survive. We came back in 1938 during the Japanese-Chinese War.

When we came back, we landed in Victoria. Like a herd of sheep, they throw us in a "Black Maria," a prison truck with wire cages. Then, we get on a boat and come to Seattle. We get off at Colman Dock. They put us in another Black Maria and took us all the way down to the back side of the immigration station. They haul us upstairs and lock us up. Every morning, it's interrogation. Now, what the hell they interrogate an 11-year-old for? Twice a day. They measure your height. Boom! Slam the board on your head. For what? They ask how many steps from your front door to your toilet? How many windows you got on the left side of your building? How many relatives on this side? Same questions every day. We couldn't look out the window. Where's our dad? My father would come down to the front end on Airport Way down there. You can't even wave at him!

We came back under a Certificate of Identity, the Department of Labor. If you are a common laborer, you cannot come to the United States, so you have to be a merchant. This Certificate of Identity is something that we had when we were born, but nobody honored it. Here's my birth certificate. I should be able to walk off the boat! We are citizens. But this is how they treat citizens. We were there for seven days, I think. My mother was there for about four weeks.

In the old days, you don't have that many people in Chinatown to start out with. The Japanese people on one side of us, and the Filipino people sort of intermingle with both sides. And when you walk down the street, you say hello to everybody. It's a real friendly atmosphere – there's no animosity whatsoever or anything. Peaceful, nice and quiet. You never see anybody fight in the streets. You could leave your door open 24 hours a day. We had only one police officer in Chinatown, but he could take care of the whole Chinatown.

I graduated in 1953 from the UW [University of Washington] in mining and industrial design. When I applied for a job in mining, the application said, "We do not accept Chinese." No Orientals. I had to change my field from mining to industrial design. I went freelance. I had to walk all over town to get one job, and people were not accepting design that well in the old days. If they could use a paper bag to pack something, why should they put a design on it? Costs extra money.

My grandfather started the noodle factory in 1917. Then about 1930 – '29, '30 – somewhere around there, my dad came out from New York to help him out. My grandfather's smart. He took off and stayed back in China when we came back. My father and his first cousin took over in 1937. My brother, Henry, and I bought the partnership in 1957. My father and his partner were getting too old. They wanted to quit. Typical Chinese. They wanted to leave the name on the storefront so the relatives and all the people they know have a place to go. We sell to restaurants mostly. The majority of our business, maybe 60 or 70 percent, is institutional and the rest is chain store and grocery.

My nephew, Tim, and his cousin, Brian, we sort of let them loose. See how far they will go. It's up to them. They seem to get along real fine with each other and they're getting things done. Maybe not as knowledgeable as they should be. Eventually, someone's going to take over. It might as well be your own people.

Walter Chinn

Born August 22, 1914, Oakland, California

We moved up to Seattle when I was a small baby with my three older brothers. At first, we lived in Canton Alley. Where Four Seas is now, there used to be a playfield, and we usually played down there. We played baseball and football and all that. And bordering on King Street, there was a little garden, not very big. They called it the Quong Tuck Garden.

My family all went back to China in 1932. I think I lacked another semester before I graduate from high school. Our dad's wish was for us to learn Chinese. We went to school there, and it was pretty hard to learn Chinese when you're 18, 19 years old. It just don't click, you know. We were in Hong Kong and we weren't segregated like some of them who went to Canton to learn. We attended school with little dinky kids.

The following year, my mother wanted us to get married. I didn't want to because I got no means of support. But she was just crying down my back, so I gave in to her. I met my wife through the same school. She lived upstairs, and we rented the downstairs flat. That way, her sister was the go-between between her and I.

My brother's wives were mostly picked. They never met them or anything. Mother picked them out and then they came over. My brothers, Harry, Mike, and I got married on the same day.

The first son, James, was born in 1934. Later, my other boy, Robert, was born. I left in '36 to come over here. I found work and sent money back. A couple years later, I decided to bring my wife over.

A U.S. citizen cannot bring his wife over. The only way to get her over – have you heard of paper son and paper girl? My wife came over as a maiden, single. I had to buy a false paper for her to come over, under an assumed name. I paid $1,400 in those days – just the paper. The reason is that they're afraid if you bring them over, they would keep multiplying. They didn't want any more Orientals. They keep the wives back there.

When she came over, we got married here to make it legal, even though we had two children, James and Robert. It's a funny situation when you can't bring your wife over. You can bring the kids over, but who's going to raise them when you're out working?

Walter Chinn ran the China Cab Company in Chinatown from 1946 to 1962. After he retired in 1965, he worked as a part-time bus driver for the Seattle Public Schools for 17 years.

陳夒堯

Roy Chu

Born July 18, 1928, Fow Sek Village, Toisan District, Kwangtung Province, China
Died December 19, 2002, Seattle, Washington

My father came to the U.S. before I was born. Most people came to the U.S. to make money. My grandpa came first. He worked in a laundry in New York. My first and second uncle came here after him, then my father. All brothers came.

When I was a teenager, there was the war in China, and there was no school. We were always running and hiding in the mountains, when we were running from the Japanese. We have a farm, and we'd just bring the rice, vegetables, and cook there. My grandpa had a plot of land, and we'd take the rice from there. I was scared to death. I was always sick – bad dreams – always bad dreams. The airplanes were always bombing the city. Because my village was close to the city, hear the bombs, machine guns. See the dead people after. The Japanese came three times. They take the whole town, too. One time, they stayed about three months. They take the food, everything. Kill people. Mostly after a couple months, they leave, then they come back again.

I came to America when I was 19. Me and my mother. It was different. The people were different. Things were better than China. Everybody had jobs.

Born in Toisan District, China, Roy Chu lived through the Japanese occupation and later joined the rest of his family in Seattle in 1947. He worked at the Hong Kong Restaurant and enjoyed singing Chinese opera.

Tek Wong

Born January 25, 1924, Toisan District, Kwangtung Province, China

The war just started. I came in 1938, the height of the young age group like my age coming over. In the immigration, there were 300 youths from my age, and they put us in four different rooms for rooming – you sleep there – and then you go to the main dining. Pretty much like in the army. Each room housed bunk beds, 40 to 60 young people, men, and then each meal we marched to the dining room. Some are married men with the wife back there in China. Most of us were youth in the teens. I was there two months waiting for my turn to be questioned.

You supposed to have one set of questions for both the father here and new immigrants coming in and to match same answer when the questions were put to you by the immigration officer. They were both supposed to have the same answer. In other words, same answer by the father and the assumed son. They could ask you how many doors in your house. You were supposed to say four. If there is a conflict, discrepancy, then you're in trouble.

Many of them bring over coaching papers, up to the immigration door, and then next day they destroy it. Some of them, they smuggle it in, and they have to dispose of it later. In other words, they still have to cram for that, they keep it longer.

When my time came and I went through, I think it was two sessions, first and the second. It was pretty smooth for me. I'm pretty much set. In other words, it's true. My father said just tell the truth. At the third one, then I saw my father was at the end of the hall, so then I was told to pack up things and I can leave.

Tek Wong came to America in 1938 after a 22-day voyage. He opened and owned many restaurants and businesses and was a charter member of the Chinatown Chamber of Commerce. He retired in 1994. He is pictured here with his two daughters.

James Wong

Born July 9, 1913, Mong Dai Village, Toisan District, Kwangtung Province, China

My father was in United States. He owned a restaurant in Wisconsin. He goes back to China to visit my family every so often – maybe every few years – and then stay in China with the family and then come back to the United States again, then earn enough money and then make the trip, go back to China. Back and forth, every so often. My mother never came to the United States because the immigration law did not allow bringing the wife over. My mother lived all her life in a village, never came to the United States.

I came from Hong Kong and arrived in Seattle in 1939. Because the Japanese invaded China, the schools closed and I don't want to move inland. My father wrote me and asked me to come to the United States. When I first came, it was a strange place, a new country. I don't know anything. All tall buildings and lots of automobiles – not like back in China.

I first came in and go to the immigration office and stay there for 10 days until they finally permitted us to leave. They ask you your father's name, your brother's name, where you live, how your village looks like, lot of questions regarding you and your family and your father and brothers, where you go to school, how your house looks like to find out if you are telling the truth. They match up what the other brother say or your father say to find out that you are the son of your father.

Right now, I'm working with the Chinese Information and Service Center to provide information, assistance and referral to the neediest members of Seattle's Asian community – new immigrants and Chinese elderly who speak very little English and have difficulties finding jobs. I am doing some translations and helping them to get services – like going to see a doctor, filling out forms and getting benefits.

James Wong ran a grocery store in Portage Bay, Washington for 15 years. After he sold the store, he worked at the Chinese Information and Service Center until he retired in 1991.

黃光夏

Henry Louie

Born December 1, 1916, Thlom Woh Village, Toisan District, Kwangtung Province, China

My mother didn't come here. She was in the village. She couldn't come here because she didn't have the proper papers – merchant papers. Only if you had a birth certificate could you come here. That was the rule in America. I came here to America in 1934. My father was over here. I was out of the immigration station fairly quickly. I was there about one week. They interrogated me. Every kind of question. They asked you what the village was like, how many houses it had, who you knew. I wasn't scared. There were a lot of other Chinese like me up there. It was like jail. They were all Chinese in this room. There were some who were older, some who were younger. They were mostly younger, about my age. There were guards looking over you while you ate. They were fearful that the Chinese would share question and answer sheets.

The Luck Ngi Musical Club opened in 1938. There were 10 to 20 people in the beginning. Japan had attacked China. There were a lot of refugees in China. In the old days, there was the Ning Yeung Association. It was a place where all the people from the Toisan area gathered. There were newspapers and books for people to read. We read about the refugees. We thought, "Wouldn't it be good to have performances and raise money to help these refugees?" Every month, we would hold one fundraiser and send the proceeds back to China to help. Some people came from out of town. Some came from the local area. Each fundraiser would raise at least several thousand in American dollars.

I like music very much. I practiced on my own. I bought records and books. I watched and I listened. That's how I learned. I also learned to play the saxophone from the white Americans. I took lessons. When I was learning to play the saxophone, I went upstairs and closed all the windows. I was afraid I would create a commotion for other people. With the laundry, around dinnertime, I would close. If I had time, I would come down to the Club and practice, then go home. When I was drafted for the Navy, I brought my saxophone with me and played dance music in the officers' clubs. I like the saxophone the best. I learned to play the saxophone first. Later, I learned to play the Chinese instruments. I wanted to learn all the instruments. I can play almost all of them. If you come from China, you're so far away from your village. You're not used to being in America, so you're always thinking about China. That's why I learned music – so that I will not forget my home and where I came from.

Henry Louie was one of the founding members of the Luck Ngi Musical Club in 1938. He was drafted into the Navy during World War II. Due to his musical background, he played dance music with his saxophone at many officers' clubs. Louie later worked at the Hong Kong Restaurant, retiring in 1980.

Fannie Eng Lung

Born March 1, 1896, Port Townsend, Washington
Died March 25, 1997, Seattle, Washington

My mother was a picture bride. She came over when she was 16. My father was here. He sent a picture of himself in his youth, and then when she came over, she saw his hair was all white. They struggled, and I used to struggle with them. I helped my mother look after my brothers and sisters. I helped with the household and did some cooking.

My mother wanted me to go to school — to learn something. I wanted my children to go to school. I wanted them to be something, to have a worthwhile life, make a name for themselves. I don't care what they do as long as what they're doing is doing good.

Fannie Eng Lung's father was one of the earliest Chinese merchants in the Northwest. She was the first Chinese woman born in Port Townsend, Washington.

Violette Chan

Born July 23, 1898, San Francisco, California
Died February 20, 1993, Seattle, Washington

Violette Chan was raised by her mother in San Francisco's Chinatown. After marrying Jick Chan, they moved to Detroit, Michigan, then later to Seattle.

Because whorehouses don't allow girls to go in, my mother dressed me as a boy until I was eight years old. When I was little, I was always hanging onto my mother in the whorehouse, where she combed hair. She had to take me along. Nobody was home to watch me.

One head took about three-quarters of an hour – sometimes longer, depending on how much jewelry they wore. They wore about $200 worth of jewelry in their hair. Real gold. Mother combed all kinds of hair. Some had a long tail, and she put colored thread in them. That took almost an hour and a half to comb. She was famous because down in San Francisco, nobody else could comb a head that don't hurt.

The girls, they were pretty girls. They wore silk dresses and tops and pants. Some were pretty young, too. Most of those girls had no mother. Some man bought them and shipped them over from China. Bought them from poor families. No boys. All girls. Used them as whorehouse girls. Some were willing to do it, some were tricked. You know, they must have known some friend or somebody who said, "Oh, I'll take you to America, you find a job, make a good life."

Mother always said to me, "If I die suddenly, don't go to no relatives. Go in the mission home." When she was young, she was at the Presbyterian mission home for two years. Her parents tried to marry her off to an old man, so she ran away and went to that home. And oh, the teachers spoiled her. They got dozens of girls. She's the only Chinese girl that could speak English and help them out in the home. She spoke English well. She was very sociable. And she's a fighter. When I was small, if girls got rough with me, I got rough back. Just like mother said, "Fight them back! Don't come home and cry."

Louise Yook

Born November 9, 1908, Swatow, Kwangtung Province, China

We came over when I was six months old. My father had already been in America. He came back to Swatow. My sister was two and a half, and I was six months, and my mother, we came with him back to America. My mother said it was 32 days on the boat. Her mother was so afraid she'd be seasick, but she said, oh, that was the best trip she ever had. She enjoyed it. But when she got to America of course she couldn't speak any of the Chinese – she only spoke the Swatow dialect – and she didn't know English either. She had four brothers, two older and two younger. They all lived in the same compound – four brothers and their wives – and they all told her, "How lucky you are! You're going over to America with the land of gold and you'll have everything so nice over there." Then she came here and she found that it wasn't so.

It was a hard life, living in Fragraria [Washington]. My father had already left us for New York. He'd always say he was going to farm. He'd start some place, then get tired. He liked the big city better than Seattle. My father said, "Your mother is a business woman and she'll manage." My mother was left to take care of us.

My mother picked strawberries. I went with her to pick, and I would carry the boxes back to the shed. I was about eight years old. We had a small farm with turkeys and chickens and blackberries. My mother raised the chickens, killed them and shipped them to Seattle to sell. We didn't seem to suffer too much.

From 1950 to 1974, Louise Yook taught kindergarten in three different Seattle Public Schools. She was the first Asian American teacher hired by the School District.

Nellie Chinn Woo

Born March 8, 1917, Seattle, Washington

I born in Seattle on Jackson Street. That time everybody delivered in the home. When 1919, we went back to China. Then that time, real bad for smallpox. That's why the three of us – I got older sister, Annie, and my brother, Andrew, and I number three – we get back in the village, all have small signs. My grandfather keep saying we already have a shot in the States, and we don't need any shot, so we got it. After we got smallpox, we would feel so bad, we would stay in the house. Don't want to go outside, see anybody. When you came back from the States, you look so nice looking, and after, you get sick. We have a real bad feeling when we're back there.

1924, we move from the village and stay in Canton until '27, and we came back to Seattle. Then we only stay one year. We said, oh, I think we'll go back China, go to finish college before we come back. My father first is very upset about you guys just came back one year and then you want to go back. But we didn't ask his position. I tell everybody, "Oh, we go back to China on Saturday." I tell all the people on a Monday – and it was for Saturday. My father said, "Okay, if you guys want to go now, never come back again if you don't like it here." I said, "We don't care. We like China." So the three of us – my brother, my sister – we take a boat and go back to China.

Nellie Chinn Woo has been a long time member of the Chong Wa Benevolent Association where she helped new immigrants learn English. She also is a member of the Jade Guild, a Chinese women's service organization in Seattle.

Following his service in the U.S. Army during World War II, James Mar returned home to Seattle to continue his father's business, Yick Fung & Company, now one of the oldest Chinese businesses in Seattle. Mar also became funeral director for the Chinese community, a role he continues to perform to this day.

James Mar

Born July 11, 1914, Seattle, Washington

I don't believe there is another funeral director of Chinese descent that is operating even now. It wasn't easy doing this thing because Chinese do not participate in this sort of industry. You have to do everything for them. Get pallbearers for them, get a minister for them, pick out the plot for them, wrap up the coins for them, write the thank you cards.

They're afraid once they talk about it, they're going to die. Chinese especially, when they go to a hospital, go to a nursing home, they think they're not coming back any more. So a lot of them refrain from going there. I think it's only within the last 10 or 12 years that the Chinese would actually come and talk to me of dying and what has to be done. They know the plots are getting scarce now.

My parents ran Yick Fung Company, an importing and exporting firm in the International District. My dad arrived here in 1909 and he started the business in 1913. We took over the business when my dad passed away.

We're more or less a wholesaler, so we supplied all the merchandise, equipment and stuff conducive to operating a restaurant. We were also agents for the Blue Funnel Line. Our ships would run once a month, and all the people from the United States who wanted to go back to China and had just limited funds would come and utilize our steamship company because it was a lot cheaper than our two competitors.

The beds were stacked 10 high, steerage class. And for those that could afford it, we had 12 cabins on the ship. Livestock was kept on the deck and were slaughtered as the need presented itself. We had pigs, we had chicken. I think the only thing we didn't have were cows.

Since we had an average of about 85 passengers every month, there was a need for someone to transport their baggage and a need to haul the passengers. So my dad started a Yick Fung Express Company run by one of my brothers, and the China Cab Company was run by one of my older brothers. Also, these people had to be fed and housed, so at our store, we had cots on the second floor, which was provided for them to wait two or three days before the ship leaves. And we also had a kitchen here with a cook who supplied two meals a day, nine in the morning and 4:30 in the evening. I think my dad thought about covering all the bases, and I think we did, as far as assisting the passengers during their short stay here in Seattle, before their departure for the Orient.

Most of our passengers, when they come here, they're going back home to die. I would think maybe less than 10 percent would be coming back. In those days, females weren't allowed to come because of the Exclusion Act, so they make these trips periodically, but most of the time, it's a one shot deal.

The reason why I'm still here is because it's a place for my brother, Howard, to hang his hat. He's single. We are more or less just keeping track of the customers that pay us on time. There's competition for us, but we don't care. We don't need it anymore.

Look at my son. He's a dentist. I would be just tickled to death if he came back down here and worked in the store. I got a ready-made job for him. You take a Caucasian. If he's a dentist, he wants his son to be a dentist, take over his practice, and the same thing with the physicians and the lawyers. I thought maybe my son might. I more or less forced him to come down every summer to pick up Chinese and talk to the Chinese people, but after middle school, he's gone.

Loy Hugh Locke

Born November 27, 1916, Olympia, Washington

I can't tell you exactly the date my father came to Olympia, but I do know that he came to this country in 1854 at age 17 with a group of railroad workers. He was known to be honest and the rest of the workers entrusted in him their pay. He didn't have to work very hard. He was more or less their bookkeeper, taking care of their money over the years.

Because of his particular advantage of having so much cash, even before the '20s, he kept it in a big large metal box. Mr. Lord of the Olympia Capital Bank used to joke with my father. He said, "Sam, you have more cash than I have." He started by investing in properties and he built the so-called Chinatown in Olympia on Water Street. Four large boarding houses where all these single men rented rooms. He owns all the buildings. He built them. He owns them.

Most of the Lockes resorted to his help. The Lockes are a small clan. They were, more or less, overshadowed by the Chins and the Wongs in Seattle, so my father and a group of Lockes set up in Olympia. In the old days, Olympia was all Lockes. I can't tell you how many but probably several hundred at first. They were laundrymen; they worked on oyster beds; they were laborers, houseboys. All single men except two families, the Kay family, who are actually Lockes, and our family. Those early lives were really tough. The basic philosophy is go to work, save every penny, and as soon as they have enough, they go back home, back to the village to get married and raise children, come back and make some more money, go back and enjoy a year or two. And that's the cycle. Until the end – they go back home to rest and to die. Wait to die.

My father came to work and make money to support his family back home. Then he had to build up his own business. My dad's first marriage was in the village – an older woman with bound feet. She couldn't travel. My mother is the second marriage. By the time he's ready to get married again, he's already in his 40s. My father brought my mother over in 1902. She raised nine children for my father – five boys and four girls.

We lived upstairs, above the stores. My early impressions of those days were not really that favorable. The anti-Chinese sentiment was so bad. The kids at schools, they were calling us dirty names. I was one of those that fought back and I got dismissed twice from school. The first five years, we attended a Catholic school, and to our surprise, the Sisters helped the other boys against us. Later, we went to Lincoln Grade School and then we were sent to China to study Chinese. Two of my brothers finished college and myself and others finished high school in Shanghai, Nanking, and then we came back. My father is the first to send all the boys to China to study Chinese so that they, in the future, could enjoy the best of two worlds. We're bicultural.

Loy Hugh Locke is the son of Sam Fun Locke, an early pioneer merchant and leader of the Chinese community in Olympia. In 1942, Locke graduated from the University of Washington with a degree in liberal arts. He worked for many years as a federal employee. He served as president of the Locke Association for five years. He has two daughters and a son.

In 1878, Bill Kay's grandparents came to Olympia and became one of the first Chinese families to settle in the area. Kay and his wife, Toy, operated Kay's Café for many years. Now retired, he is an honorary member of the Rotary Club of Olympia, along with Governor Gary Locke.

Bill Kay

Born October 15, 1916, Olympia, Washington

My father came over when he was a teenager, probably around 14 years old at that time. My grandfather was already here working as a cook in a logging camp. My father went back to China in about 1914 or 1915, and he got married and then he brought my mother over. My older brother was born in China and came with my mother, and then they established a family here in Olympia.

There were no Chinese families in Olympia except for our family and Hugh Locke's family. Most of them were just single men. They had lived in the Chinatown, which was composed of three grocery stores and had living quarters upstairs – rooms that the store owners rented out to these single men. For all these single men who came back from work, there'd be a kitchen in the back of the store where everybody cooked their own meals. These stores catered to them for all their foodstuffs.

Chinatown was located on Water Street, between Fourth and Fifth, which is presently where the Elks building is, right across the street from where the lake is. At that time, it was just tide flats. The water from the bay came in and the tide came in, and it was all water underneath there.

I'm a member of the Locke Association. If an immigrant came over from a village or the same area as the other Lockes were, they could always depend on the association to give them a hand, like going through a lot of problems that required somebody to translate for them or do whatever to help them out.

As far as I can see, the older fellows had already established themselves in Olympia at these storefronts, apartments and rooms – it was kind of a place where they could gather. Of course, if you're a Locke, when they came over here, they tend to bunch up with their own cousins or uncles or relatives. They just kind of stuck together here. Different towns and different cities have different families. I think if you're a small clan, you tend to get off someplace and establish your own self there instead of trying to fight the larger organizations.

Priscilla Chong Jue has worked for many years as a textile and woodblock artist. She and her first husband, artist Fay Chong, raised three children. She later married Willard Jue, a prominent Chinese American community historian.

Priscilla Chong Jue

Born November 30, 1916, Fragraria, Washington

I was born in a little town in Washington across the Sound. It's called Fragraria. It happened to be on a Thanksgiving morning. I found out I was nameless for two months. Every day when my older sister went to school, the teacher would ask her, "And how is the nameless baby?" Finally, my father told her to tell her teacher to name the baby. That's how I came to be Priscilla.

My parents were both from Swatow. My father came over first. He came actually to study. He wanted to study medicine, but then he got involved with the Chinese Baptist Mission. The Baptist went to Swatow first, and his grandmother was the first convert. So he came over more or less with their approval, and when they needed somebody at the Chinese Baptist Church, he became a minister. He was there a number of years.

My mother came over 1909, the year of the Alaska-Yukon Exposition. She was a very enterprising woman. She had grown up in a store. Her parents had a store, and Swatow was a seaport. When the ships would come in, they would be so busy. They sold everything that anyone would need – socks, umbrellas, hats and various things – so it was in her blood. Coming over to see the Expo, she was really fascinated with it, so when we had a chance to go to the Puyallup fair, she decided she wanted a booth there. I think it was 1931 or so. She also had a store downtown. It was called Chinese Embroidery Shop. Her brothers sent her merchandise from Swatow, so she didn't need much capital to begin with and then when she sold things, then she could repay them and ask them to send more. It was very unusual, especially since she didn't speak English much. She was a good saleslady, and then there was always one or two of us kids helping. I'd get out of school to go over and help her. We all helped there. We were all kids growing up in the store.

During the Depression, we ate a lot of peanuts and lettuce. We bought five heads of lettuce for a dime before closing time at the market on Saturdays. My mother cooked lots of peanuts with rice and soy sauce. To this day, I don't enjoy cooked lettuce.

Anne Chinn Wing

Born March 9, 1919, Seattle, Washington

I was born in the first Chinatown in Seattle. It was located at Second and Washington Street. At that time, most of the families – and a great deal of them were Chins – came to the Northwest and they would come through my father's store at 219 Washington Street.

We had our home at the back of the store. The store was a very busy place because at that time, there were so few families and mostly single men. Because they couldn't speak English and they were unable to get employment, that was the core of their everyday activities.

Anne Chinn Wing's father, Chinn Kee, was one of the first Chinese employed by the Immigration and Naturalization Service. Wing has a long history of community involvement, especially in the arena of human relations. She helped organize the Chinatown Chamber of Commerce Queen Pageant for over 30 years.

When I was very young, I remember that one of the highlights of our life was preparing for the Chinese New Year. It was a big event. My mother would clean the house and she would get all the food in because she didn't believe you did any menial work during the Chinese New Year, and the broom was put away.

The house had elaborate hangings over the doorways, especially over the entry table. The hangings were bordered with tiny glass mirrors. The reason they had those little mirrors was in case anything unpleasant like the devil showed up, they would look in the mirror and it would be so bad that it would scare them away. Before every dinner, she would burn firecrackers, and we were taught to speak the sayings bringing good luck for the New Year, and we would jump for joy.

I can remember our living room. The wall had this long line of pictures of all the family, of my father, and the chairs were around the edge of the walls. We were taught when people came in that you greeted them, and you always told them to sit down and you always served a cup of tea and you always served it with two hands. It was a form of courtesy. And if you were sitting on a chair and an adult was standing, you would be tapped on the head to be reminded that you were to give your chair to the adults. When they punished you, they tapped you on the head. Chinese would call it *len gok tay*, the tap on the head. And sometimes the tap wasn't a tap, it was a good hard knock. So I had a lot of *len gok tay* when I was growing up. We were taught to have manners. We were taught to respect the elders.

I am quite distressed because so many of the young people today, they live their own lives. They've forgotten about their culture. I'm very involved in the family association, and we find that so many of the young people can't be bothered with the family association. But we had the family associations because it was a point where all the different families who came here in the early years could come and congregate. And they could share family traditions and family holidays and problems. And you could help each other. But I can count on my fingers, sometimes not even that, the number of young people who come to the different functions, and they're forced to come. When I see young people, I always say to them, "Try to speak and write your language because it's going to mean a lot to you."

I would like the future generation to be interested in their culture, interested in their traditions, because if you look in the mirror every day, you can see the color of your skin and the color of your hair and you should be very proud of it. And if you haven't become proud of it, you should see why. You probably haven't delved into it enough or participated in the many facets of your culture. I would like to instill that into the next generation and to their children – to be proud of their culture.

Henry H. Woo

Born May 19, 1907, Seattle, Washington
Died March 26, 2001, Los Angeles, California

The Wa Chong Company was the largest business in Seattle. They did export, import, shipped a lot of flour, herring, lumber, paper products to China. It was significant because they have the capital to buy the merchandise from China and Hong Kong. They have the capital to keep the merchandise. They don't have to sell it right away, and they ship it to all these places and then mostly on credit. Some of them work in the mines and railroads, they don't get paid right away, and they say, "Okay, I'll be good for it." And that's where Wa Chong comes in. They got the capital to take care of them. That's why they open the store in Butte, Montana – to take care of his workers. They would come in and says, "Okay, give me this, give me that. Give me some herbs. I'll pay you next pay day." It's how they run the business. You got to have knowledge, and you got to take chances. Like they ship 5,000 tons of herring and not get paid. You got to take a chance.

When I was 14, I moved to Wa Chong Company to help my father, until age 19. My duties were to help cook in the kitchen and help my father write letters, so he could send the letters back to the fireworks company in China. The Wa Chong Company was selling all kinds of firecrackers, shipped to smaller cities

After earning a degree at the University of Washington in 1930, Henry Woo went to China to work as a technician at the Nanking Aircraft Works. He earned the rank of Major in the Canton Air Force. During World War II, he worked in aircraft design for several government contractors in Los Angeles. After the end of the war, he was self-employed as an accountant and tax consultant in Los Angeles.

around the Northwest – Butte, Montana, Walla Walla, Yakima, Portland, Idaho. The firecracker was stored in a farm in South Seattle, and the farm was owned by the Wa Chong Company. The fireworks were located in a single warehouse, right in the middle of the farm because of the fire hazard. During the fireworks season, I would go there to help them pack up the fireworks to ship to the different customers. That was only about two months before the Fourth of July, but after that, the season is over.

People would come to the Wa Chong to see my father and ask for a job – most Chinese, Filipino, Mexicans, hired from Seattle. Average pay about $200 a season. As a cannery foreman, you get about 600 for the whole season. That's about six months. He brought over relatives from China to work in his canneries. The cannery foreman is always a Woo. Because my father never went to the canneries, he trusted his own relatives to go to Alaska, Puget Sound to take care of the cannery work.

If they've been working for my father for a period of years, he would advance their money so they would show up the next season. The next season starts in April, and it ends in August. He would advance their money because in the meantime they have no work. When the season starts in April, these men are hired. They order all their clothing that they need from the Wa Chong Company. We charge them so much, and they ship them off to Alaska. Then when the season's over, these men come back and get paid at the Wa Chong Company. Some of them wind up with nothing because, in the cannery, they have gambling after hours. These men that work, they back to Seattle, they have nothing, and they wait for the next season.

In Alaska, we live in bunkhouses. If there's full 50 people, we live in one house, all 50 people. The beds are in bunks, different layers. When the fish start coming, sometimes you work 16, 20 hours a day. No overtime. The men are paid 10 cents an hour. Before the fish start coming in, there's always a Sunday for day off, but during the season, I don't think we have any time off. We all ate the same food, Chinese cooking. The food was composed mostly of salmon and corned beef. When we go to Alaska, we buy these little pigs, and when they get to about 500, 600 pounds, we kill them, and that's all the fresh meat we had during the season.

The fish go up to the fishing elevators, and from the fish elevator, they go to a machine called the "Iron Chink." They call it "Iron Chink" because "Chink" is a slang name for Chinese. The fish goes around, and that thing cuts the head off, slits the belly. It comes out, and you have to clean the fish by hand. Then it goes through a machine that slits it in different sizes, so they can put it in the can. Put it in a can, and they go through a vacuum machine. The vacuum machine sucks the air out of a can and close the can. After it closes the can, it goes through a cooker. Cook about one hour in the cooker, and the bone and everything is cooked. They leave it to cool, then it's ready to pack, ready to label. That's the process of fish canning.

Yee Goon was 725 King Street. My father moved all his cannery business to that store because he had a disagreement with Wa Chong over financial arrangements for the canneries. It was a store occupied by the Woo family, those people that are too old, they don't have no work, they don't have no family, have no place to go, so they stay at the association for nothing. They lived there, ate there, played *mah jong*. It don't cost them anything because that's what the Chinese say, "We always take care of our own."

Helen Woo Locke

Born December 8, 1913, Seattle, Washington

My father, Woo Gen, came to Seattle about 1870. I was raised near Chinatown. Father leased several apartment dwellings on the Eighth Avenue South block and on Main Street. When I was about six years old, we moved to a larger new house. Father had bought a large lot on Main Street and built a five-bedroom house, with a vegetable garden in the back and flowers and plants in the front yard. There was also a chicken house, and we raised lots of chickens and ducks during the Great Depression, so there was no lack of food. We went up to Beacon Hill and picked berries for jam and jelly, and my brothers went fishing a lot. We also had a lot of salmon brought back from Alaska. Father died when we were very young. I remember saying good-bye to him in the steamship to the Orient. To this day, I cry every time, remembering his last words to me. He was a very good father to us all.

The first Chinese church was at an old house on Sixth and Washington Street. Then it was moved to 10th and King Street in Chinatown. The church's missionaries, Miss Skiff and Miss Snape, devoted all their time and energy to the young people of the Chinese community. Many clubs were formed for the young girls. We enjoyed picnics and camping trips. In the evening, Miss Snape had English classes for the newly arrived men from China. Miss Snape would take many of us down to visit the immigrants detained in a place down near the Pike Place Market – some as much as three years. We would talk to them, and they would cry. To cheer them up, we sang gospel songs and played simple games. It was very sad to see them confined so long.

During the Great Depression, Helen Woo Locke moved to Kowloon, Hong Kong. She returned to Seattle and worked as a tour guide in the Smith Tower. She raised five children. She is pictured at front center with her sisters in 1917.

Clifton Goon

Born January 26, 1920, Portland, Oregon

We moved to Seattle after my grandfather, Goon Dip, passed away. He was 62. Goon Dip was an original entrepreneur. He contracted to send people up to Alaska to work in the canneries. He was an original venture-capitalist, into speculative investments in gold and copper mines. He developed the Hirst-Chichagof Gold Mine in Alaska around 1920. There is a mountain in Alaska that was named after him – Mt. Goon Dip. The mountain is not too far from where the gold mine is located.

I was only 13 when he died, but I remember that he was a heavy-set man. When we were kids, he came down to Portland to visit. He would have a shot of whiskey, and he would let us dip our fingers into the whiskey. When I was growing up, he owned the Hotel Oregon in downtown Portland. My grandfather had somebody run it. He was living in Seattle in the Milwaukee Hotel. He used to have a bodyguard – a white fellow. I remember I saw him once.

After we moved to Seattle, my father took over management of the Milwaukee Hotel. He ran it for the family. After my father died, I was running the hotel, collecting rent, running errands and doing repairs on the exterior, fixing windows or the top of the building. This was from 1959 to 1965. By then, the building was starting to deteriorate. We sold the building in 1965.

After graduating from the University of Washington Pharmacy School in 1941, Clifton Goon worked at Rex Drugs in Pioneer Square and later at the West Seattle Hospital Pharmacy. He retired in 1980.

Marjorie L. Lee

Born August 6, 1916, Seattle, Washington

My grandfather, Goon Dip, was originally from Portland. My mother was born there. Then he became the first Chinese consul of Portland and Seattle. He ended up here. He lived in the Milwaukee Hotel, on most of the fourth floor. He and my grandmother and two aunties lived there until the time he passed away. They had a suite of rooms. He had a suite on one side of the fourth floor. There were about six to 10 rooms there, a whole string of them along. One room was for Mr. Brotchie, his bodyguard. Then Goon had his office with his desk and everything. Next one was his bedroom, and then combination bath. Then the next one was my grandma's bedroom, and then the one next to that was my auntie's bedroom. Across the hall was the kitchen and sort of like a dining area, where Grandpa had all his meals and Grandma did most of the cooking.

When we were living in the family home on 10th Avenue – that's before Yesler Terrace was built – I used to ride down there on

my bicycle, down to the hotel to see him. He didn't speak very much. We'd go in there and then we'd just leave him alone. He's in the office or he's in there eating. We didn't bother him at any time. He didn't really speak to us a lot the way my grandmother did. I was there quite a bit. After a while, my father forbade me to go down there on my bicycle because, you know, young ladies don't ride around Chinatown on bicycles. Later on, I drove down there and saw him quite often. I always remember I'd go in there in the afternoon, after school, and he would have an early dinner, and I remember his having steak and sliced tomatoes. Maybe a little rice, I don't know, but that's all I remember – every time, he was having steak and tomatoes.

At his funeral, I wore white shoes, white socks, white pleated skirt, a white middy and a white beret. It had to be all white. Grandchildren, they like them white like this. His funeral was at the First Presbyterian Church. It was filled to overflowing, and the people were out in the streets because they couldn't get in. The funeral procession had two bands. One was an American band, and they marched down the street. The other one was Chinese music in the back of a truck in the parade. Also, days after that, before a week in Chinese custom, we all went there to the cemetery and we ate along with my grandfather's spirit. We brought food and then we ate there supposedly with him. I haven't seen anybody do it since.

I met these girls when I was in Broadway High School. They were all from wealthy families, and they asked me to go to picnics with them. They all had bicycles and I had a bicycle, and they wanted to go on a bicycle trip. So we went with my girl scout camp, and we all went to pick up a couple of girls who lived in Broadmoor, and we got to Broadmoor, and they stopped me at the gate and everybody went in and they wouldn't let me in. The girl scout captain stayed with me and said, "Why are you doing this?" He said, "I'm sorry, but it's Caucasians only." "All right," she said, "then I'll call them." He called in to the house to ask permission to let me in. Isn't that awful? And that's one of my experiences as a young girl. If I had known any better, I wouldn't have gone then. I would have said, "No, I'll stay right here."

One summer, I was home from school, and I got a call. I went to the phone, and I said, "Hello, this is Marjorie Lew Kay. You wish to speak to me." And she said, "Yes. We want to invite you to a Rushing Tea." She said to come at a certain time and at such and such sorority. I said to myself, "Rushing Tea." I'd been around people in this society enough to know a lot of things about prejudice. So I thought for a minute, and I said, "Oh, pardon me, but you're inviting me to a Rushing Tea? Well, I just want you to know that I am a Chinese American." And she says, "Oh, just a minute please." So she came back later to the phone and said, "Oh, I'm sorry. There must have been some mistake." I said, "Yes, I realize that. That's why I told you because I want to save you embarrassment and save me embarrassment when we got there."

Marjorie Lee's grandfather was Goon Dip, the first Chinese consul of Portland and Seattle. Lee is a third generation Chinese American on her father's side. Having a great admiration for the outdoors, Lee formed Seattle's first all Chinese Girl Scouts Troop in June, 1940.

Harriett Wu

Born October 16, 1910, Hoiping District, Kwangtung Province, China
Died October 24, 1997, Seattle, Washington

I came over with my brother's wife. We both came over. I was about seven or eight. My brother was on this side. He didn't go back to get us. Both of us traveled on steerage to come to Seattle. My father was dead at that time. I don't know a thing about my father other than what I read and what people tell me about him.

Our store – the King Chong Lung Company – was the gathering place for all these workers that wanted to go to work up in the canneries. We paid for their passage, and then when they came to the store, they cooked their meals and ate together and waited for that certain day when they could go up to the canneries.

One man was a very good cook. I called him Moon-sook. God, did he make good baking powder biscuits! Sometimes, he'd have some left, and he'd put it in the cupboard. He'd tell me about it if I came into King Chong Lung to visit. He'd tell me there were some *men-bow doy* in the kitchen. I'd make a dive for the biscuits.

I remember how they all gathered in the spring, or when it was cold, they gathered around a potbellied stove and sat around the stove and spun tales of their experiences. That memory I'll never forget. They were good men, dedicated men. That was their livelihood – to go up to the canneries, save their money and come back home and use that money until it runs out. When they came back from Alaska, they gave me gold pieces that they had acquired up there.

I worked for the King County Treasurer and King County Assessor for years. I was the first Oriental to get a job in the King County courthouse. The only non-white person was a black man, and he was the starter for the elevators. So when I got in there, people were curious as to how or why I was there. Somebody asked how an Oriental deserved it. I made the point. I behaved myself – I was quiet and I fit in. My work spoke for itself. I picked up everything that they taught me. I picked up work fast. I was the first Oriental to hold a job like that. Amazing. I guess I broke the line, as it were, and then after that, they came one at a time.

Harriett Wu was the daughter of Ah King, a prominent cannery contractor who helped finance the Chinese village at the 1909 Alaska-Yukon-Pacific Exposition.

Myra Mar Chin

Born October 4, 1916, Seattle, Washington

My mom used to take in all the people who came over from China who needed a place to stay. My brothers had a lot of friends, and then people who needed a place to stay or needed some help, my dad had them come to the house. That was my dad's way of helping. My mom and dad were that way. We weren't rich, but then that's the way they lived.

I played basketball with a Chinese team. It was just a group that played basketball. We were just friends. We played at Japanese Baptist Church. We generally played against Japanese teams because we were the only Chinese team at that time. There's not many still around here that used to play. We were in early high school. I played side-center. I don't know what they call it now. It's different from the men's games, you know, before. We played until some of them left town and some got married. It's quite a few years that we played. It's a long time ago, but that's what I like to do best, to play basketball. It was fun.

The happiest time? Oh, my marriage, but then prior to that it was just having a happy family. We used to walk to the beach and go swimming a lot. We always used to go down to the lake from our house on 25th and Jackson. In those days, we could walk from our house down to Madrona or Mt. Baker, go through the woods, and come back at night. But, now you can't do that. The times have changed that much.

Myra Mar Chin and her husband, Don, opened the Sun May Company, a basketry shop in Chinatown in 1962. The business evolved into a Chinese gift shop now managed by her son, Donnie.

Raymond Chinn

Born July 11, 1925, Seattle, Washington

I was born right in Maynard Alley, down here in Chinatown. My mother and father came over in 1923 and then they rented a store space in the alley and they lived in here since. Our store was started in 1928. There used to be sort of a farmers' market right down here on Seventh and Weller. Every morning, farmers would bring trucks, produce and fruits up here. And a lot of the stores would come down and pick up fruits and vegetables and take it back to their own shops or some of them would take it back to their own carts and they would go on from here to residential areas.

Raymond Chinn is a tireless leader in the Chinatown community. By renovating his family's building, the Rex Hotel, in 1995, he hopes to spur other property owners to do likewise with vacant hotels. He is retired, but serves on the board of the Chinatown/International District Business Improvement Area.

Chinatown was quite a place in those days. So many of the families were living down in this area. On a hot summer night, the people that live up in the apartments would bring all their bamboo rattan chairs and benches, and just sit it right in front of the sidewalk. The mothers would be fanning away and the children would be running around. The fathers would be there smoking their long water pipes. We would be up until 10 or 11 o'clock playing around in the streets here. A lot of the shops would be open late, so there was lots of light around.

There was a little field where the Four Seas Restaurant is today. That was what we called our own play field. We used to go up there to play softball and touch football. In the wintertime, we would light a fire right in the middle. We dig a hole in there, and we would light up a bonfire, and we bring potatoes. And we would cover it up with mud and throw it in there and heat it up and cook it right there. We would sit around and talk, telling stories usually, ghost stories or something. It was quite memorable.

I always remember New Year's. In those days, for New Year's, my mother would clean up the whole place. We lived in the alley, but she really kept it spic-and-span and we would mop up everything. Everybody would put on their best for New Year's Day. And they are always on good terms because they want the new year to start out nice. They never reprimanded us on New Year's Day, so we get away with murder sometimes. The wives were usually all busy – making these Chinese pastries and cakes and sweets. My mother would have pictures of our ancestors and you offer them food and burn incense. They had lion dances, and of course, the *lai see* was always the fun thing. You go and visit your relatives – they all give you a little package with money in it. That was a big thing for us.

I went to Bailey Gatzert School, and I went from there to Washington Junior High School, and from there, I went to Broadway High School. Unfortunately, my dad was fatally injured in an automobile accident in 1940 and I was a freshman at the time. It's a funny thing. My mother died about five years later. These older people, after they've been married for so long, they die of a broken heart. I tried to keep the business going because I felt that my obligation was to keep the family together and to keep my dad's business together if I can, because he put so much into it. I was the oldest son. Being the oldest son, you sort of take on that obligation. At that time, my dad had three restaurants besides the store.

I had to go to part-time schooling from then on. I finished high school in 1943. One of the things I regret the most was that I couldn't go on to school. When I look back at that time, my schoolmates were considering going on to college. And here I was, my thoughts about going on to college were really nil because I was just so concerned with: "Who's going to work tomorrow? And the next day?" I had to work seven days because all the restaurants were open seven days. I never took a day off for many years.

As a child, Bill Chin lived in the Milwaukee Hotel in Chinatown. After college, he worked as an accountant at the Boeing Company for eight years, then went into business for himself in 1959 selling life insurance. He helped found the Oriental Restaurant Association in 1970 to provide health care coverage for restaurant workers.

Bill L. Chin

Born June 28, 1925, Seattle, Washington

Living in Chinatown in those days was quite a life. There was always something to do. On summer days, we used to pack a lunch. We used to climb to the top of the fire escape, sat there and ate our lunch. It was great. I used to go to all these different restaurants. I would go up the back stairs and I kind of pester the cooks. I was just a little kid then, you know. And to get rid of me, they either give me a piece of barbecued pork or a box of these chow mein noodles – crisp ones – to get rid of me.

I used to go see the cowboy movies at the Atlas Theater. One time, I went to the movies and I fell asleep. I must have slumped across the seat. I was only six or seven at the time. It was late, and I hadn't come home, so my parents must have been worried and they called the cops to go out and look for me. I remember seeing a policeman going up and down the aisle with a flashlight. I guess he must have been looking for me, but I didn't realize it at that time.

My father, Jackman Chan, was born in China and came over in 1911. The first job he had was working as a janitor at the old New Richmond Hotel, down there right across from the train station. Then he got involved in the gambling business, and one of the old-timers, Goon Dip, who took a liking to him, took him under his wings and taught him how to invest in the stock market. My father had investments in different restaurants and then he had investments in gambling and lottery houses.

At one time, when he had the gambling house, my dad could have bought Chinatown. But his biggest problem was that he liked to gamble himself. So by the time he died, he lost all his money gambling. He liquidated his stocks. He surrendered his life insurance policies. He was in real bad financial shape. You know, you can't name me one Chinese gambler that died rich. If you open a gambling house and don't gamble yourself, you can't lose.

I was drafted into the army and took basic training in Fort Riley, Kansas, which was cavalry school, and went overseas to the European Theater. By the time we got over there – I was in the 13th Armored Division – we were winning the war, so what we did was just go through the cities in Germany and pick up prisoners. Once in a while, we ran across snipers that took shots at us, and also once in a while, some of these big German 88 millimeter artillery guns got pretty close to us. That was kind of scary, too.

After we got discharged, we all went to college on the G.I. Bill. I went one year down at a small Baptist college in Oregon called Linfield College, and then after that, I finished off at Seattle University. I got my degree in finance. When I got out of college, I had ambitions to get in the investment business. I had interviews with Merrill Lynch, Dean Witter, Walston and Company. But at that time, there wasn't one Asian in the investment business. They just figured they weren't ready for a Chinese. Today, it's a lot different. Job opportunities are much more open for Asians now. We had it rough, but then our fathers and grandfathers had it even rougher. Those old-timers really had it rough.

Being in the insurance business, I know a lot of people. The only thing I regret is the fact that you pay the price because when you work night and day, day and night, you're away from your family. You spend more time with your business than you do with your own children. You miss seeing your children grow up.

Mary Luke Woo

Born April 26, 1918, Seattle, Washington

My dad and mom had the import and export business at the Bow Lung Company on Eighth Avenue South. It was a Chinese store where they sold dried foodstuff. It was headquarters for people coming to the States or going from the States to China. My father took care of people going from and to China, helped them through immigration. We had to get rooms for them, like at the Mar Hotel, but they ate at our store. We had meals for everybody who came and left. Then we helped them move to the train station or the boat or wherever they're going to leave or arrive from.

We lived in the store. It was very crowded. Our whole family lived in the back room. In the 1930s, we renovated the second story and our family lived up there. In those years, we were considered kind of well-to-do because my dad was supposed to be in a good business. All my life I've been lucky to always have food. I don't have all the luxuries, but it was a good childhood for me.

In those days, young girls weren't supposed to go to Chinatown. Not very many girls wander around Chinatown. But it was peaceful. When we were young, a bunch of girls, we just walked up and down the street at nights, and we never worry about any trouble or anybody attacking us or anything.

First, I went to Bailey Gatzert, and then I went to Central School, then I went to Franklin High School. When I graduated, my mom and dad wanted me to go to University of Washington, but I thought in those days, girls don't have to have so much education, so I said let my brothers go. So my brothers both went to the University of Washington. My younger brother was a pharmacist, the first Chinese American pharmacist in Seattle, and he opened Luke's Pharmacy. My younger brother started his pharmacy up in Summit Avenue, then later he moved down to Chinatown.

My older brother went to medical school and he became a doctor, the first American-Chinese doctor in Seattle. He came back to Seattle and he opened his office right at the same store that we grew up in. The Chinese people who couldn't afford to pay him, he just gave him medical advice and treatment free. My brother had good bedside manner, and he took care of them and explained to them in Chinese what medicine is good. People should know that they did a good service for the Chinese community.

During her 20s, Mary Luke Woo played center for the Chinese Girl Athletics, the only Chinese girls basketball team in Seattle at the time. She also was one of the first Chinese Americans to work for the City of Seattle. She was employed by the Seattle Police Department for 25 years.

Josephine Chinn Woo's father, Chin Fook Hing, owned a knitting factory in Chinatown and was the first Chinese to serve as a juror in King County Superior Court.

Josephine Chinn Woo

Born January 16, 1919, Seattle, Washington

My father had a store on the corner of Seventh and King. It was a dry goods store. You name it and he sells it. In the back, we had a few knitting machines. It was like a small knitting factory, and he would sell sweaters, too. Hairy, knit wool sweaters, and people who go to China would buy it and take to China. He also sold Chinese phonograph records. My mother helped out in the store. My mother was illiterate. She could not read or write English or Chinese. We had these boxes of records written in Chinese on the shelves. She had it all memorized. Anybody want to buy a record, she knew just where to get it.

We lived in the back there until I was nine years old. There was a storefront with a showcase counter on the left side. My brother slept there on the floor. He would put his bedding between the wall and the showcase. In the back, we had a little eating area, and behind that, a partition for where we slept. My mother used to cook the dinner in the basement, and when it was ready, she would carry it upstairs in a big tray. My father had a building built on 12th and King when I was about nine, and we moved up there, but we still spent most of the time down in Chinatown.

In those days, it was safe all over. Nowadays, you don't let your kids out of sight, but in those days, we just played all over with all our friends without supervision. I would go to Canton Alley, Maynard Alley. There were a lot of vacant lots around that area, and we just played all over. We played house and hide and seek and things like that. I remember one time we went to the Chinese store and bought some ginger to eat, you know, the very hot red ginger, and we pretended that was our dinner. We ate that and we all got sick.

We went to the regular American school, and then we went to the Chinese school, from four to seven. It was difficult to go to two schools. It was quite hard. We had reading and writing. We recited and we learned to write with a brush. We learned to read a lot of food phrases. I was not a scholar. I used to do my American homework under the desk. I went five years. Of course, I'm glad I went now because a lot of it stayed with me. I lost a lot, but it helped.

I went to Bailey Gatzert, then I went to Central School, which I think is no longer there, and then I went to Franklin High School. In those days, I thought that there was not too much sense in going to college because friends that I know who had gone to college ended up being waitresses. We couldn't get jobs in offices, in Caucasian places. And if you get some lowly job in a department store, that was real hot stuff. My friends were waitresses in Chinatown.

Rose Chinn Wong

Born April 2, 1925, Seattle, Washington

We were quite well-known in Chinatown because there was a gang of us. There were eight of us. If there was any noise in Chinatown on Eighth Avenue, they probably would say, "*Chou Yee jai nui.*" They'd say, "Oh, it's just Chou Yee's kids." We were known as Chou Yee's kids. If we did anything wrong, it was "Chou Yee's kids, Chou Yee's daughter or Chou Yee's son who did this" – you know, snitching. Then it would come to my father, and my father would say to my mother, "Your daughter, or your oldest son, or your third son, or your oldest daughter did this! Take care of it." And Mom would glare at whoever it was. She would say, "Don't do it," and she would give us what we called "the eye – *gao ngan*." She would *gao ngan*, and then we'd say, "Uh-oh."

My father spoke English. My mother spoke very little, but she knew the right words to say. If somebody came to the door and complained about us – that we were stopping traffic because we were out in the middle of Eighth Avenue playing baseball – they would say, "What do you do with your kids?" She would say, "What's wrong with you? You shouldn't be driving." I'd say, "Mom, what'd you say?" and she'd say, "I don't know." "Well, what did you tell the guy?" She'd say, "I don't know." I'd say, "I heard you said this," and she just laughed. She wouldn't admit to it, but she knew English. She would put on that old style Chinese old lady act, which was a riot. She'd be yelling at us in English sometimes. Somebody would knock on the door, Mom would go to the door, "What?" They'd say, "Miss, you want some?" and she'd say, "No speak English!" Bam! She'd close the door. We'd turn to her and say, "You big liar." She'd say, "Well, he should've known better to knock on my door."

My mom stayed at home, raised us all, and she was just plain mom. She never went anywhere. In fact, the only time she ever really broke out of her chosen spot, shall we say, was when all of us left, we married. Then she got acquainted with some of her friends, her old cronies. They would go play *mah jong* here, or *mah jong* there, or *mah jong* at her place. We were all grown and gone, so she occupied herself that way, which was great because what she did was she became independent of us. We were independent of her already, but she became independent of us. Up until the point that we left home married, we were always "Chou Yee's daughters" or "Chou Yee's sons," but when we all left, then it was just mom.

When Pop brought her over, he placed her in that place on 507 Eighth South and we wanted her to move. One day, my younger brother called me and said, "Hey, we gotta' get her out of Chinatown." I said, "Don't ask me. What did she say? Talk to her first!" So then he called me a few days later and said, "You knew what you were talking about." Mom said, "Your father brought me over. He put me here. And when I die, he'll know where to come and get me." I love that phrase because when she died, she was in the place, in Chinatown, where all of us were born, and Pop came and got her. I think that's a great love story, don't you?

Rose Chinn Wong grew up in Chinatown with her many sisters and brothers. Her uncle was a founder of the Wa Chong Company.

Paul Louie

Born September 10, 1918, Seattle, Washington

Louie Loy was my dad. He was born in China in 1862, and entered the United States at Portland, Oregon in 1882 at age 20. He was baptized in Portland in 1887 in the Methodist Episcopal Church when he was 25 years old. He was know as *yeh so loy* – a "Jesus boy" or "Christian boy" – because of his being with the mission. By the time I grew up, he was up in years. When I knew him, he was in his 60s. I didn't even know that he spoke English until after he died – until Willard Jue told me one day. My dad and I never spoke two words together in English – just some Chinese, and even in Chinese, it was very little. Most likely he learned English at the church. My memory of my dad is very, very dim.

I grew up in Canton Alley. All the houses there – tenement areas – were full. There was no empty spot. The Depression was pretty bad. In the morning, we would go down to where the produce growers have empty wood crates and I would break up some of that stuff and bring it home for firewood. And we had Hooverville down near the waterfront. In terms of supplementing our food, we were able to get surplus or leftover food from some of the restaurants. I think a number of families in Canton Alley may have been like us, but one of the things is that while many of us were "poor," we were not destitute, which was quite different. Even though it was hand-to-mouth, we made do, and we were fortunate in that respect.

I attended Bailey Gatzert Elementary School, Washington Elementary School and Garfield High. In those days, the Chinese Baptist Church had what they call "home missionaries." These were women, and they make contacts with the families. We had a kindergarten, and that's where the kids went for a year or two before going to public school. I got into the youth program there – kind of a high school group. Through scholarship help by the Chinese Baptist Church youth advisor, I attended Linfield College in McMinnville, Oregon, graduating in 1942. It's a Baptist school. I went on to Harvard Divinity School with a scholarship and graduated there in June, 1945 with a degree, now recognized as a Master of Divinity degree. I was among the first group of Americans of Chinese ancestry who went to seminary in the States.

After I finished, I was with the New York Chinese Presbyterian Church as the youth advisor, part-time. I was also working with one of the Chinese Chinatown banks. It was less than a year. Then I went back to Seattle because my dad had passed away, and I thought that with my mother getting along, I should go back. I went back around 1947, working part-time as a youth worker at the Chinese Baptist Church. The Seattle District of the Baptist Association of the Northern Baptist Convention, now American Baptist Convention, ordained me into the Christian ministry in 1948.

Our generation was very fortunate. One of my older sisters had a couple of years of college. I was the first one in my family to have gone through college all the way and have a college degree, so we were very fortunate in that way. I think opportunity emerged. I was making contacts outside of Chinatown.

Paul Louie's ministerial work took him down to California in 1949. From 1951 to 1955, he was pastor of the Oakland Chinese Presbyterian Church. He served as Christian education minister at different Presbyterian churches in Berkeley, Davis, La Canada and San Fernando until 1969. He is an active Board Member of the San Francisco Chinese Historical Society.

Jeni Dong Mar

Born November 21, 1928, San Francisco, California

We lived in 6 Canton Alley. It was the first apartment. We had the front, which you would probably consider the front of a store, as our living area, and then right beyond that was a fairly good-sized area that was a kitchen, a bathroom, and then there was an upstairs and that was where our sleeping quarters were. At the end of the building, there's a stairwell that led upstairs to the building and then there were about four units. Sometimes our parents would send us up there to do errands or give messages, and I hated it because it was so dark and spooky. The hallways would have one bulb of light and that was about it. Even though my parents would say to our face that there is no such thing as ghosts, at night we used to lay in bed and hear them talk about ghosts.

Jeni Dong Mar has fond childhood memories of participating in Girl Scout Troop 75, Chinese Baptist Church, Chong Wa Language School, and riding on the Chinatown float in one of the Seafair Parades. Photo early 1930s.

My father, typical of those days, was about 20 years older than my mother was. I never really felt there was any communication between our parents. It's like my mother did her own thing with her friends, and my father would go out and do his own thing. I remember him going to the canneries. He'd be gone all summer. Neither one of them spoke English much, if at all. I think later on, my mother understood more than she actually spoke, but I never felt that my father understood and he never really did speak English.

There's really no communication with your parents the way we know it now. We can discuss things with our children now, but in the old days, you just didn't. My mother was very, very strict. You just didn't discuss anything with her. In fact, as we grew older, it was just understood that once you walked through the door, you weren't allowed to even speak English – we had to speak Chinese.

I really want my children to know. It's history. It is part of my past. If we don't keep it up and pass this on, it's going to be totally lost among the younger generation. It's even more important because of interracial marriages that they are having now. I have one daughter who's married to a Caucasian. He's a wonderful son-in-law and I have a wonderful granddaughter, but I want her to know that she's part Chinese. I want them to understand a lot of this tradition. I don't want them to lose it. In Chinese tradition, family life is so important. I really want them to inherit a lot of that, rather than thinking of themselves as individual and not as a family core. If anything my mother and father passed on to us was importance of family. You had this father figure and mother figure, and even though we were really poor, it held us together.

James Louie is best known as "Toney," derived from his Chinese-speaking name, Toun Doui. He grew up in Canton Alley to a self-educated entrepreneur father in his 60s who managed a garment-sewing factory on Second and Yesler and was working on his own Chinese-English dictionary. Louie currently lives in Berkeley, California and is enjoying retirement from being an architect.

雷純泉

James Louie

Born May 23, 1925, Seattle, Washington

My dad came over in the late 1800s. He was the youngest of two or three sons that fled from the famine in China. He sort of ran away from home. He operated the garment factories and sewing factories down on Second and Yesler in the 1900s. By the time I was born, he was in his 60s. There was a large age differential there, so I really didn't know him as a father but more as a grandfather. We never played baseball together or played catch or any of that. We just respected his age. We never talked much, but when I was in Los Angeles in 1943, I wrote my father a letter in English, and he replied in English. I was so flabbergasted. I felt so good. That was a real contact, a communication of any sort and any depth. He was about 82 at the time. I knew he was in failing health and asked him how he was. He wrote back saying he was doing fine, asked me how I was doing, that type of thing. Within a few months, he passed away.

I grew up in Canton Alley, number 4. Chinese Garden – they had a band on weekends. We had to listen to the band until two o'clock in the morning every weekend. The kitchen of King Fur Café was across the street from us, so we would hear that, we'd hear garbage cans all night. Beyond the alley, and across the alley from the Chinese school, used to be an open area. It used to be gardens for some of the people from Canton Alley and Eighth Avenue, who had their own plots where they grew vegetables. We had a plot where my mother grew *gai choy* and *bok choy*. My mother would clean it, package it – pack it means getting string and tying around in bunches – and I would put them in the basket. I'd walk through Chinatown, up and down the streets. You had to sell it to the businesses. They would have workers and they would cook lunch, dinner for the workers. We would sell them the vegetables to use as soup. They would be our best customers. If I had six, eight or nine bunches, they'd say, "Oh, we'll take the whole bunch for the soup of the day tomorrow." And that's great because I don't have to sell anymore. What I did, I hated it. You know, kids, you don't want to go around selling vegetables.

Each of the families would have a store that was started by their family. Kwan On Wing is so-called the "Louie store." I used to hang around there as a kid because it was safe – it was Louie store – and they all welcomed me to play. Kwan On Wing used to make tofu in the back. Everyday at three o'clock the tofu was ready, so if I got there at three o'clock, they would give me a bowl of *tofu fa*, put a little sugar on it, and I would get a snack. It was great! I also used to go there and play Chinese dominos. I learned how to play real well against the old men. I used to play and beat all those guys.

They were mostly single adults, male, Chinese who sat there. Most were waiters, laundrymen, retired or cannery. If they were in cannery, they made enough during the run in Alaska so they can live off that for the rest of the year. They were not married. They'd just have a single room in one of the upstairs buildings. They don't spend very much. The rooms were relatively inexpensive, and their needs are not that great. We didn't have a lot of stuff, so there wasn't a lot of stuff to spend money on.

Born in Canton Alley, Chinatown, William Eng grew up working in his father's knitting store, hand laundry and Chinese restaurant. After high school, he worked as a machinist at the Boeing Company for 39 years, retiring in 1987. He restores Corvettes in his spare time.

William Eng

Born December 7, 1929, Seattle, Washington

My mother was a housewife and my dad had a knitting store at 625 King Street. He went to school to learn to machine knit. They sold sweaters and, you know, haberdashery. They had shirts, underwear, scissors, knives, nail clippers, fountain pens, soap, et cetera. They had everything there.

We used to make bean sprouts years ago – one of the first in Seattle. That was my mom's part of the business. She made bean sprouts at home with tubs, cans and watering troughs. Needed 200 square feet of area to grow the sprouts. Back then, we only sold it for a nickel a pound. Part of our chores was to deliver to the restaurants in Chinatown, so we knew all the people and all the stores in Chinatown back in those days.

My brothers and I used to have a shoeshine business called Three Brothers Shoeshine. I was 10, Nelson was eight and Tuck was six. We'd charge five cents a shine. We'd start in the International District and work our way down to First and Occidental. The people used to like how Tuck shined the shoes because he was so cute doing it. So Nelson and I just carried, lugged the stuff and Tuck would shine.

Back then, we'd shine a couple of shoes and have enough money to buy two hamburgers for a nickel each. The patty was five inches in diameter and three-quarters of an inch thick with all the condiments. We'd have two burgers and wouldn't have to eat the rest of the day.

We went to Bailey Gatzert. When you went to school, you didn't want to say you had rice for breakfast. They ask you and you sort of make up and say you had cereal or something like that. So we said we had milk and toast or cereal. In reality we had rice – but you know, that's cereal! You just didn't want to go into deep explanation of what you ate. You're afraid of the ethnic thing, and at that time they would say, "Yuck, what do you eat that for?"

We used to go to school and then come back and go to Chinese school from four o'clock to seven o'clock at night. You didn't hardly have time to do school work. There's always something to do. You had to deliver stuff before we went to Chinese school. Back in those days, just to heat the house, first you had to move the wood. After, we'd have to carry coal. It's not like turning on the furnace with a button like that. We were just kids then, but we used to have to work hard.

My parents were really strict. "You do this, or else!" They say, "Jump." You say, "How high?" You don't question them. I come to the realization you don't have to treat your kids that way. To keep your kids in line, they don't need that much pressure. I always told my kids, "Hey, you want a spankin'? I'll give you one anytime, but I prefer that we be able to sit here and talk about it. But anytime you want a spankin', I can sure give you one if you want one!" I don't think I raised a hand with any of the kids. Maybe I swat them once in a while on the butt, but not the kind of thrashin' we used to get!

Winnie Tuai

Born May 10, 1926, Seattle, Washington
Died January 16, 1997, Seattle, Washington

Dad, he is the quiet man in the family in China. Does not reprimand children. Mom is the – what do you call it? – matriarch. She raises the family, and she does the scolding and all that. Whenever we got beatings, my mom always saved it up. After maybe a month or a couple weeks, she'd say, "Okay, line up." Eldest to youngest, and then she'd get her – they call it *saw hong,* a feather stick. She'd go down the line, and she'd say, "This is for what you did this day, that day, that day!" And she would just go on down the line.

Dad never raised his voice. He loved baseball games, and I used to go with Dad to the Rainiers down there on Sick's Stadium. He wanted company and I'd go with him. He was working as an herbalist, you know, Chinese herbs. Whoever needed something to cure whatever ails them, he'd pick up all those different herbs and pack them together. He worked in Wa Chong.

Mom cooked a full meal before she sent us off to school. We had rice, we had vegetables and meat and everything before we went to school. Talk about a heavy breakfast! Then when it came to dinnertime, Dad would be the only one that got meat. We would eat veggies and all that. But Dad, if he had pork chops, whoever was able to grab first got the bone to gnaw on.

Winnie Eng married Liem Tuai after a very brief courtship. They were married for 46 years and had three sons. She is pictured here in 1956 with her son.

Jessie Edwards

Born August 19, 1905, Astoria, Oregon
Died 2000, Seattle, Washington

My parents landed in San Francisco, California. They came up to Astoria by covered wagon. My father panned for gold in the mountains of California. Then he became a blacksmith and shoed horses in the Rogue River Valley. He was known as "Blacksmith Jim." In Astoria, he got a job at the Flavel mansion, turning on the heat in the morning and washing the windows in the daytime. My mother was a housewife. They had 10 kids.

I had a happy childhood. We went horseback riding up to the hills, went to the beach, turned rocks to look for crabs. We hung a tire from a rope and jumped from it from high places, and it swung way out. My mother had ducks and one goose that chased after us. She had chickens and a pet kitty, so gray and cute and friendly. We had one dog, Roger, a beautiful brown and tan police dog. Used to take him to the river and throw sticks. My brothers used to go hunting for ducks. According to the season, they went deer hunting with friends.

My husband, William, and I met because we were the only younger people in Astoria. He was a newcomer from Chicago. We took notice of any newcomers. We got married back in Chicago. We moved a lot. We went to Minneapolis, Las Vegas, and then William went to Los Angeles because his cousin was living there then. Helped run a restaurant there. We went to Spokane and ran another restaurant. That didn't do good. We went back to Astoria again because we had a hard time. It was the Depression. William had a hard time finding work. We had nothing. It was awful. I had to work in the canneries. I received the salmon when the launch brought it in, then weighed the fish, dumped the fish on the floor, then went up the trough to grade the fish. I had an important job. That's why I know fish really well. Silverside steelhead and Chinook were the best.

Jessie Edwards was one of 10 children born to James Y. Howe (Houi Yem Chow) and Daisy How (Toy). Later in life, Edwards worked in the Bumble Bee cannery as a salmon dock receiver where she met her second husband, Percival Carlos Edwards. Her first husband was William Sims (Woon Sim) who died in 1954.

"Pudge," as most of his family and friends called him, started work when he was 13 years old at Tai Tung Restaurant. His later jobs included working at New Luck Toy restaurant, Chinook Ferry and Trader Vic's Restaurant. He later became the first Chinese American to enter management at the U.S. Postal Service in the lower 48 states. He was also an avid sports enthusiast and helped found the Seattle Mixed League Bowling Club (1953) and Seattle Chinese Athletic Association (SCAA).

Wallace "Pudge" Eng

Born April 2, 1931, Seattle, Washington
Died September 5, 2002, Seattle, Washington

My family lived here in this house for 61 years. My mother came over from China. My dad brought her over in 1920, and she lived there until she died in 1981. My mom and dad raised eight children here. We had the upstairs also. I don't know how they did it. This place was actually quite small, but it was home.

Whenever we were sick, we'd come in to Quong Tuck. They had a doctor. He was a Chinese herbal doctor. He would feel the pulse, examined you for a while, then he would write out a Chinese prescription. You'd take it to Wa Chong or any other herb place, and they'd fill that out for you. He would always put some raisins into the package, too, to kind of sweeten the taste because that tea that came from that prescription was really hard tasting.

Back in the '30s and '40s, Wa Chong was very prosperous. They had the walls lined with drawers, each one of the drawers having different types of medicine in it. On the right hand side, they had a colander with more drawers of medicine. They had the old type of rollers for crushing the different medicines. They had all the kind of toys that I, as a kid, would look at, but wasn't able to touch, such as water pipes. In the basement, they had this big machine. They made noodles. They had a drying room. They had rice and everything else piled up there. They had a mezzanine up above that you could look down, and up there, there was more medicine. They had firework sales up the street here on 10th Avenue. They had a garage that was stored with fireworks that they would bring down here and sell. They also had a farm out in Georgetown that had a big warehouse where they had fireworks, firecrackers, rockets, toy guns.

The face of Chinatown may not have changed, but the spirit of Chinatown has changed quite a bit. This used to be a meeting place for people, but there's no such thing anymore. People are just all scattered and they all have different interests now. They have their own families. They have their own businesses. They have their own lives. There isn't that unity, the continuity like you would think. Every time I come into Chinatown I feel sad because it used to be so friendly, so safe. I used to be able to walk out at night and not have a worry in the world. My sisters could walk in the dark, and there'd be no problems. But I remember maybe about 20 years ago, coming down into Chinatown and right in Canton Alley, I heard an old man yelling. He was obviously getting mugged, so we yelled and the perpetrator ran south. This was Chinatown and this was happening in my town and that bothered me.

Henry Chin

Born July 16, 1901, Nan Chong Village, Sai Chuck, Toisan District, Kwangtung Province, China
Died November 18, 1991, Seattle, Washington

Chinatown, no cement. All wood! Down on Seventh, Eighth Avenue, all the street – just wood. One piece of wood, two piece of wood – and there's a big walk. One day, it's raining and I fall down in the street and I see money, 40 dollar. I take that 40 dollar to my father. "Goddamn. You go and steal money!" I said, "No. I fall down. The money is still wet. So I pick it up." My father give me hell. "You go and steal some of their money." I said, "No, I just fall down. I pick it up. The money is still wet."

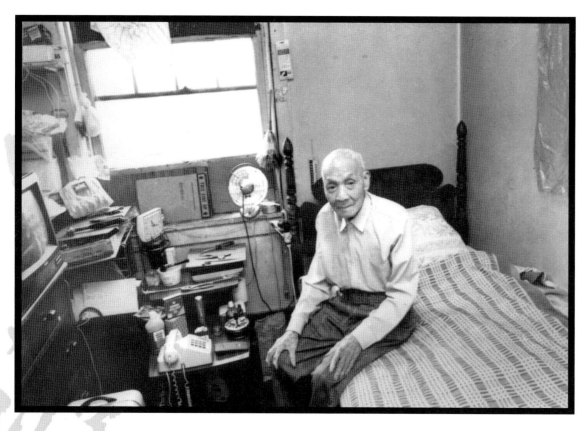

Henry Chin worked as a cook in many Chinatown and downtown restaurants. He continued to work well into his 80s.

Andrew Chinn

Born June 27, 1915, Seattle, Washington
Died January 9, 1996, Seattle, Washington

Andrew Chinn retired after working 31 years in production illustration at the Boeing Company. He was an original member of the Chinese Art Club, a Chinatown organization started in 1936. He taught watercolor painting for many years.

Some of our friends, they paint. I watched them paint. That's how it got started. Later on, we had lessons, but at first, I just watched my friends paint. Some did oil, acrylics, some did these tempera watercolors.

In 1936, we organized an art club. It was called *Toong Sing* – the Same Voice. The Art Club met each month here on Jackson Street. We had a group of parents that encouraged us along. They were the ones that furnished the space, the necessary funds for the prizewinners. You show your work. Everybody encouraged everybody. We did a lot of painting – mostly watercolor, some oil – later a few pieces of sculpture. We had a show every month.

Henry Kay Lock

Born October 10, 1910, Sun On Village, Toisan District, Kwangtung Province, China
Died July 20, 1992, Seattle, Washington

During the Depression, my dad was working at the Hankow Café on Jackson Street and I got a job as a waiter, working 12 hours a day for $40 a month. Not only waiter, but janitor and window washer and delivery boy. I put in a couple of years there, and when he went back to Olympia for our restaurant, I took over his job as cook and continued to work there for two or more years.

Then, Harry Mar and I rented a car and we went into our own taxi service. Mr. Chin had a big, old Studebaker and we rented it for $25 a day and we went into business. We had no name, it was private. We didn't have a license or anything. We just ran it in Chinatown for the sporting houses and the girls. We did that for a year or so and then I went to work for Baby Hong at the Oriental Cab Company. I worked for him for about three years or so.

Henry Kay Lock, known by many as "TV Lock," was an expert in television and hi-fi technology. He was also self-trained in photography. From 1949 to 1961, he worked as a quality control inspector at the Boeing Company. He later worked at Magnolia Hi-Fi until he retired. Lock was president of the Locke Association for many years. He also served as English Secretary for the Bing Kung Tong. Photo early 1950s.

Morton Woo was the labor contractor for Libby McNeill & Libby Cannery. He hired all the help. There were probably 20 to 25 Chinese and a few Filipinos, and when they got up there, they would hire a few locals as well. The stores and supplies were furnished by *lo fan* [white] firms. The Chinese foods were supplied by Wah Young and Ah King's. We would go in late spring, and would go by boat to the Kenai Peninsula, which took about five days.

They had bunk houses and one big house for the dining room and kitchen where all the help ate. I usually stayed two-and-a-half to three months. Spent the whole season and would come back with around $200 to $250. It wasn't too bad. It was all hand labor. You cleaned the fish and threw it on the line, which took it to the cutting machine and it chopped the head off and split it and then it moves to the section where it's cut into pieces for the can. We ate pretty good – got lots of salmon to eat.

Chinatown at that time was really a busy, bustling place with all the gambling houses open. There were four houses: Mei Jew, Wah Mee and two owned by Hop Sing down on Second Avenue. There were lots of lottery joints. The police were mostly paid off. I remember Charlie Louie used to be the payoff man. He took care of the gambling joints and paid them off.

The gambling business supported quite a few people. It always seemed that there was a little money floating around. No one seemed to go hungry. It's funny, but during the Depression, the *lo fan* had bread lines and soup lines, but the Chinese always took care of their own. We had three big tongs – Hop Sing, Bing Kung and Hip Sing – and everyone was a member of the tong. Every day, there was a free dinner and everyone got something to eat.

When I tried to bring the family over, it took over five years to get them. First, the people in the Hong Kong Consul Office that takes care of the visas and all that tried to get money to push their papers through. They approached my wife and asked for $400. They tried to scare you and sent a couple of guys to where you are living and go through your house to see what materials they can find to work against you. They went through the house and got letters and pictures and tell you that's not your son and that's not your daughter. Finally, they sent the kids over, saying that they were mine, but they held up my wife's case. Our attorney finally got them to send the wife over for trial here. So we went up to the Federal Court in Tacoma. Joe Locke was our interpreter, and when the judge asked one of the kids whether I was their father or did they have another father, Joe said to the judge, "Who ever heard of a kid having two fathers?" The judge laughed and cleared the case, and after five years, we finally got the family together.

Henry Hing

Born June 28, 1914, Seattle, Washington

My dad's store is right on the corner. We're talking about King Street now, King and Seventh. It is a general merchandise and knitting factory – knit woolen sweaters, sleeve and sleeveless. The Dollar Steamship Line, it's all run mostly by Chinese in the cooking division or stevedore or the likes, and being Chinese citizen, they can't come ashore to Seattle. So every time the ship docks at Smith's Cove, which is about 10 to 12 miles from here, he would have two suitcases, one on each hand, and nighttime after the store closed, he would take a taxi and take a suitcase filled with sweaters and all the toothpaste, toothbrush and things of that nature to the Chinese on the ship that couldn't come aboard.

He closed the store up every Sunday, and he take the family around to Leschi Park or Volunteer Park or Washington Park. I remembered one time he took us out towards Ballard to the Government Locks, and either the people or kids, they threw rocks at us up in the window of the trolley. Somehow that scared

me, and much later he told me of these incidents, and I remembered them. It was, you know, prejudice. Same as when I was at the University of Washington. I would sit down in a barbershop on the main avenue, and I sat there and sat there for a half hour while all the other people come in and they sit down and get their haircut. Then I spoke up, and they said, "We don't service Orientals." I don't go uptown to get my haircut anymore after that. It's so I get my haircut down in Chinatown by Filipinos. Same thing in Portland. There was a group of us went there. We go sit down for a cup of coffee, and no waitress came to give us a menu or anything. We asked, "Can we have a cup of coffee?" They said, "We don't give service to Orientals." We walked out. Said you can't win. No use making sense out of it.

I used to work in the cannery, bookkeeper. That was back in 1934 to 1939. What I worked in the summer month was enough money for me to go to school with, and I don't have to depend on my parents. It's a one-line cannery. It is just one line going from where the fish is butchered to the cooking area. Two-line means they have two lines going, doing the same thing. Three years after I worked there, I went to another cannery, Port Althrop. We were about 100 miles from Juneau. I was managing the upstairs cannery, the canning division. We take the sheet metal, put it into the machine, and then it rounds it off and makes cans with it, put the bottom on, and it shoots down to the first floor. We were on the second floor, and there's a conveyor belt that takes it down to the first floor where they do the actual canning. There were always more Filipinos going to do that type of work than Chinese. I say about 75 percent are Filipinos, 25 percent Chinese.

Those were pretty fun days. Some day, we take a company boat and go fishing on our own. We take a nail, pound it down and bend it, make a sort of barb out of it. We tied it to strings and we try to catch salmon. I remember one time we were out fishing, looking for crabs. They were so plentiful. We take a spear and caught a hundred of them. We called up the Filipino cook, and I said how about coming down and make some crab for us. All he had to do was boil it. We gave him part of the crab for his work and we kept the rest. We had a crab feast. At the end of the season, if they have a good season, they give us a case of salmon to take home – dented ones, not the good ones. So we take the best salmon we can get there and we put the dent in ourselves. You always get by doing things.

Henry Hing worked at the Boeing Company as a technical illustrator for 26 1/2 years. He has two daughters, Sherry and Trina, and currently resides in Burlingame, California with his wife, Pearl.

Nancy Jang was one of the first women in Seattle to learn how to drive a car. She did this at the urging of her father who needed her to run errands after her mother passed away. At the age of 50, Jang went to college and earned a Bachelor of Science degree in Business Administration in just two years.

鄭陳瑞銀

Nancy Jang

Born December 6, 1926, Seattle, Washington

My dad came over about 1920 under the sponsorship of one of the relatives, who bought him papers to come to the United States. He came over and then tried to establish himself in some kind of business, but I guess he wasn't very lucky at that time because the Depression started. He did whatever he could. He used to deliver coal by the buckets, carry it up to the different apartment houses and try to earn some money that way.

I remember the Depression. It was very hard. We didn't have much of anything. There were a lot of things we could not afford. In those days, they used to deliver ice. The iceman would come around and he'd chip the ice, and we'd eat that. There was tar on the street, and we used to pick up some of that and chew it. You couldn't afford to buy gum, so you'd chew the tar.

The butcher around the corner, I guess he felt sorry for us because we're a big family. We couldn't afford to buy meat because meat was rationed and he would give us free hotdogs now and then as a treat. Across the street was a doughnut shop. They had a lot of rejected doughnuts that didn't quite make it and we'd get a lot of doughnuts.

We ran a laundry on Pike Street, 13th and Pike. There were seven of us living in the laundry and there was only three bedrooms, one small kitchen in the back and one drying room in the back. We had a storefront where people brought their laundry. I'd be ironing after the American school, which was from eight to 3:30, and then after that, I went to Chinese school from four to seven. After that, I would come home and iron clothes until midnight every night. Calluses on my hand. When you're a young kid, you don't care, just get the work done. It was very hard work.

Up the street on 16th and Pine, there was a theater there called the Venetian Theater. After 10 o'clock, my mom and I used to go to a show all the time, and we'd get in free. The manager knew us and was very nice. He said, "After 10 o'clock, you can just come on in."

They were talking movies. A lot of romantic shows. Anything we could see for free because we didn't have a radio and we didn't have a TV in those days. All we had was a phonograph, the kind you wind by hand.

In the old days, we knew everybody. I miss that. You walk down the street and you say, "Hi, Greg" or "Hi, Ron." You just knew everybody that walked down the street. There has been so many people that have immigrated to the area. We just don't know anybody anymore. There are a few old-timers that are still running the stores. They're all old friends. But I miss running into people more often on the streets. I think the older generation is getting too old. They're all dying off or they're moving off to the suburbs where nobody ever sees them anymore.

Bruce Dong

Born August 6, 1931, Seattle, Washington

My father worked with my grandfather in their local business – the Tientsin Trading Company – a curio store, in the sense that they sold Chinese artifacts and things of this sort. They had investments in property, too. My mother was a typical homemaker, stayed in the home and did the usual domestic things. I guess I would call it a typical immigrant home. The parents were good at providing the material things, making sure you were well fed and clothed, but as far as communication is concerned – sharing thoughts and getting counsel about the future – I did not get any of that. That's probably one of my big regrets. Not the warm personal relationship. I don't fault my parents for that. They were under a handicap being immigrants to the U.S. They were always very busy working hard. Their language, their culture probably produced a chasm between their children who were more Americanized as they grew up here.

I grew up in a house located on the corner of 20th Avenue and Fir Street, in the Central District. When we first moved there, it was a predominantly Jewish district. My childhood friends were

predominantly Jewish. Most of the Chinese at that time lived in what is now called the International District. We were probably the exception at that time. My grandfather was very prominent in the community, and I'm guessing that it was by his choice to buy a house outside the International District because he could afford it or was sufficiently well-to-do.

I was sent to Chinese school, but being a typical kid, I kind of resented that. I did not enjoy Chinese school. The Chinese school bus would come by our house and pick us up around four, after we got out of regular school. It took us to the Chinese school in Chong Wa in Chinatown, and then school lasted from four to seven. So that made for a long day for us. But at the same time, we enjoyed playing with each other and playing flashlight tag and all the other little games that kids enjoy.

Another difficulty is that the Chinese school that we went to used Cantonese as the medium of teaching, and at home, we spoke Toisanese. The two dialects are sufficiently different where they are not mutually compatible with each other. I remember I thought, "How come at Chinese school we say this, and at home we say that?" No one really bothered to tell me, and I guess I was just too shy or too ignorant to try to pursue why there was a difference in dialect.

Because most of my friends were Jewish, I had mixed feelings about my racial and cultural identity. I don't think it was necessarily negative, but it did not help to develop in me a strong appreciation of the Chinese culture at that time. I did go to Chinese school and had contact with Chinese friends and the Chinese community in that way, but it's just like going to school away from home. You see them at Chinese school, but you don't see them for the rest of the day.

I really didn't have any close Chinese friends until I became active in the Boy Scouts, which was a troop sponsored by the Chinese Baptist Church. It was a very fun experience for me. I really enjoyed the activities – jamborees, camps, learning how to tie knots, that sort of thing.

I remember what a good man Willard Jue was, who was the leader of the scouts. He and his wife, they were very kind to us and took us to a lot of things and did a lot that my own parents were unable to do because of their own background. It was simply because of geography and because of the sponsorship of this particular troop that all the kids happened to be Chinese. But I don't think that we Chinese ever thought that we were better or worse than any other group. We just happened to be Chinese, and it helped to develop our sense of pride in being Chinese. I thought that was very good.

Bruce Dong received his master's degree in political science from the University of Washington. He taught American history and world history during a 33-year career as a teacher in the Seattle Public Schools. He spent over 10 years at Franklin High School and over 10 years at Queen Anne High School. In his classes, Dong introduced the study of foreign languages. He retired in 1993.

Guay Lee

Born 1914, Toisan District, Kwangtung Province, China
Died October 14, 1998, Seattle, Washington

When I first came to America, I went to school to learn English. I did part-time jobs. At four or five o'clock in the morning, before it was light, I got up and went to Virginia Mason Hospital to work in the kitchen. I worked for three or so hours, then went to school. I also went to night class at church to study. I read so much that my two eyes were tired. I only made two dollars per month. So you can see, no big money at that time.

Once I finished these four years of school, I came out and started doing accounting. This uncle introduced me to start working at the Wah Young Company. When I first came to Wah Young, I was bookkeeper. After I did that for one or two years, then I became manager and looked after the business. I've been at Wah Young for over 60 years.

If you're in business, you have to have patience. Otherwise, you won't be able to manage. You will have customers that will

say things you don't like. You just ignore what they say. The customer is always right. Let him talk. It doesn't hurt me.

When I was small, I always wanted to be a big merchant. I don't think I made it, but I did my best. When I came over to this side of the world, I didn't have any spare time. Other people, they all were trying to find a place to play, but I was constantly thinking about working. I had to put food on the table and study, so I had little time.

When I was a small boy in China, I was with my uncles when they were selling a cow. To buy a cow back then, you had to pay $180. That was a lot of money. The buyer only gave a small amount because he was very poor. He proceeded to lead the cow away. I asked my uncles, "Is that all they're going to pay?" My uncles told me not to worry because they would bring the rest of the money when they had it. Their word was good.

In the old days, it was the same way in America. For example, if I sold you a cow for $150 and you only gave me a penny and led the cow away that same day, I was confident that I would get the rest of the money later. I know this is true because my uncles did business this way with Americans.

Now, people are a thousand times smarter than people were before. They get more education than an old man like me. But we stuck by our word. Today, people sign a contract and it doesn't mean anything. People nowadays are what you might call "too smart."

Let me tell you how it used to be. The price of things used to be cheap. Now, with inflation, everything is very expensive. I used to do all this work – five or six hours in one day. I got two dollars. Nowadays, people won't even put in an hour of work for two dollars. When I came to Seattle, there were not even 3,000 Chinese people, but now, in the state of Washington, there are 160,000 people of Chinese ancestry. When I came, there was one 42-story building, the Smith Tower. Look at all the buildings now – 50, 60, 70 stories tall.

My children have a lot of advantages I did not have. I was 15 years old when I left my home, not able to see my parents at all. I was on my own. Do you know how hard that is? I had to do so much work. If you have your parents behind you, they can help you with everything. My boys, they didn't have to go to school and work at the same time. My boys were very lucky. I wasn't lucky.

In 1929, Guay Lee came to Seattle. After completing business school, he began working at the Wah Young Company, an import-export business founded in 1910. His community service included over 10 years as president of the Chong Wa Benevolent Association and over 10 years as president of the Lee Family Association.

Ben Woo worked as an architect from 1955 to 1983. He served as director of the Chinatown-International District Preservation and Development Authority from 1983 to 1989. He retired from his last job as the director of the King County Department of Construction and Facilities Management. He helped found the Chinese Community Service Organization, Wing Luke Asian Museum and Kin On Nursing Home.

Ben Woo

Born June 15, 1923, Seattle, Washington

When I was eight years old, my father decided our future belonged in China. He decided that we would all move to China and grow up there and be educated there as real Chinese. So he sold everything he could sell, took all his money, and shipped us out to China. We sailed on March 18, 1931. Instead of going home to the village, he went to where he thought the business opportunities were, and that was in Shanghai. We lived in a little colony out of Shanghai that were all people from Toisan. He built a house and brought his first family up there, and then my mother and all of us kids also lived in that house. There was not a lot of peace in the house, so later that summer, my father bought some property in the next village, closer to Shanghai where there was a university. He hoped that we would grow up there and eventually attend that university.

That fall, Japan invaded Manchuria and attacked Shanghai to teach the Chinese a lesson. They shelled the old part of the city, where my father had invested all his money. We gathered our belongings and fled to a small village, and when it was determined that it was safe, we went back to Shanghai and lived in the French Settlement. We ended up being very poor. All of us were sick, especially Mary who had a wracking cough. George and Raymond lay burning with fever. George recovered, losing all of his hair and shedding all of his skin. Mary and Raymond were buried in Shanghai. My father haunted the American Consulate in Shanghai to seek an entry permit because he had earlier surrendered his right to re-enter the U.S. The only reason we were able to come back to the United States was that all of us kids were citizens. We landed off the President Jefferson on Memorial Day, 1932.

My folks opened a laundry out on Queen Anne Avenue. I was nine then, and that's where I started to adjust to America again. I went to Warren Avenue Grade School, then to Queen Anne High School. The daily routine involved no dawdling after school, but directly home to work in the laundry. We did all the stuff. Customers bring all their dirty stuff, we sort it out, put the marks on it, write up the ticket. Then you send the dirty stuff off to the wet wash, a large commercial laundry. When it comes back, we take all this tangled mass and we'd shake it out. After we sorted it out, we starched it, then we would hang it up in a little room, which was heated by a gas heater. It was a drying room where there was really no ventilation. You would dry the clothes and all the moisture went into the air, and then you lived there in that air. You lived in the back of the laundry.

I always felt more than a little deprived during my teens. Where other kids were free to participate in school activities, being poor and being Chinese and having to share in the laundry work seemed very unfair. There was a lot of racism during that period. At least once a week you were accosted and told to go back where you came from. Even kindly people like my teachers would, in all friendliness, tell me I should work hard and get a good education and go back home to China to "help my own people."

When I was young, the Chinese community was very uniform in its makeup. They were all people from Toisan. They were all members of the club. It wasn't until the late 1940s before anybody started coming in from North China, from Hong Kong, from other parts of China.

Completely different outlooks – more modern, more economically well off, more educated. They didn't carry the cultural baggage that the people from the village did. Now, you have all kinds of mobility. You can live where you want. You work where you want. It's not a community anymore.

Hing Y. Chinn

Born January 4, 1912, Mai Gong Village, Hoiping District, Kwangtung Province, China
Died March 5, 2003, Seattle, Washington

I was born in China. After my father got married and I was born, I never saw my father. He came over this country and tried to make some money. Back in China, I lived in a village, and nothing in the village, all surrounded by rice fields. It's this little village, and then a big, big timber all around it. Nobody can get in, because in China, in the old day, a lot of bandit. If they see a kid, they take the kids away and sell it to somebody. That's why we were just like a prisoner in China, living in the village. Maybe about 60 people, surrounded by all rice fields. That's how I lived. There was no store, nothing. The store's about a mile away. If you wanted something special, you have to travel. We hardly have any meat. All we have was the vegetables we grew in there, and that's all. Whatever we raised, we'd eat. That's how people lived in China in those days. If you wanted some meat, the big butcher

Hing Chinn ran the China Garage in Chinatown for about 10 years, until the beginning of World War II. He then worked for the U.S. Postal Service as Post Office Supervisor in the auto repair shop in Seattle until his retirement in 1973.

would come down once a week or once in two weeks, but in those days, people have got no money to buy meat anyhow. The reason we had a little money because my dad used to send my ma some money so often. The money come in rolls, my ma so happy. When I was thinking about that, what I told my ma is that, "Ma, when I grow up, when I make money, I will send you money like that."

I came over this country. I was 10 years old. When I was going to school, you know what happened? You know what they do to me? They put me in first grade. The first grade only five to six. When I go into the room, I can't even stick my leg under the table because I'm so doggone big. I was 10 years old already, you know what I mean? Two years later, there's a class come up. They call Opportunity School, out in Broadway. It is run like a high school. They have a special English class, special math class. They got different kind of trade. Well, I said when I came over this country at that time, hey, I don't want to spend so much time in school. I want to go over to this country and make money. I said okay, I'd like to transfer to that school. So I take five subjects. After I go there for two years – I was in fourth grade – the four to five teachers that work on me, they said hey, you qualified to go to high school. Hey, even though I don't hardly know very much, I was happy. I want to finish school.

One day, I happen to talk to this machine shop teacher. He said, "Hey, Hing, what are you going to do when you graduate from high school?" In those days, I see a lot of friends, they go through college, they cannot get job anyhow, so I make up my mind, I don't want to go. Anyhow, I fooled around with cars.

So I said, "Well, I'd like to go learn how to be an automobile mechanic." He said, "You want to do that? I know they have an auto mechanic class at Broadway. I know the teacher over there, and if you want to go, I'll introduce you." So one day, after school, that teacher took me in his car to Broadway and introduced the teacher over there. He tutored me, and then the following year, I went to the automotive school. That was a two-year course.

When I finished school, I was pretty brave. I wanted to open a garage myself. You know where the Wing Luke Museum building is? That used to be my garage. It's a storage garage – people keep their car there for storage. The Filipinos used to come, and then they leave their car in the garage so they can go to Alaska for the cannery season. After about two or three months, they come back and take their car. And I would have a repair shop in the back. I would have a couple of gas pumps, to pump with the hand and sell gas to my friends. We were still experimenting in those days. We tried to do everything. Even though we're not good on bodywork, we're going to take the job. It's a real good experience. I rented that thing for over 10 years.

In order to survive, when you work for yourself, you have to work at least six days a week. When you work for the government, all you do is work five days a week, eight hours a day. When you're on your own, you probably work about 10 to 12 hours a day. And after you finish up, you got to go home and do a lot of bookkeeping. All those bookkeeping drive you crazy. And then with the government, you don't have to collect the bills.

Melvin Woo

Born February 18, 1917, Seattle, Washington

When I was six, I returned to China. My father was sick, so all the family moved back to China. He died when I was 12 years old. I came back in 1933. There wasn't much work then. It was Depression time. I only went to Pacific School for a little over a year, not more than two years. I go to school in the daytime, and then after school, I went to the laundry and worked. In those days, 80 or 90 percent of the Chinese are in the laundry business. I stayed there and went to school. The guy that owned the laundry gave me a couple dollars a week for spending money – lunch money.

The only time I worked in a Chinatown restaurant was during the wartime. I think it was '43. I worked at the New Chinatown Restaurant – Sixth and Main corner. I managed the dining room. After the War, I went to Mt. Vernon. I went there in '49, and I was there for 33 years. I ran a restaurant – Shanghai – for 33 years. I operated four of them altogether in those 33 years. One is pretty good size, and the other three were kind of small. These were all the same name. Different from restaurants in Chinatown. Not many Chinese in Mt. Vernon. I hired three or four Chinese. Most of the waitresses were *lo fan* [white].

In 1982, after 33 years of working at his Shanghai Restaurants, Melvin Woo moved back to Seattle's Chinatown, where he remains today. He and his wife, Chin Chen Lu, raised one boy and two girls.

Wilma C. Woo

Born October 6, 1925, Seattle, Washington

The New Chinatown was known as a bottle club – you bring your bottle of liquor and they sell mixers for you. Kind of an after-hours club, with dancing and open until five o'clock in the morning. I started out as a cashier, and then, one by one, the bartenders leave. They couldn't handle it. At the last minute, I went into the bar with no knowledge of how to make drinks – none whatsoever – because I don't drink. But I have to learn the hard way. If I didn't know, I call somebody to tell me how to make it. That's how I became the bartender. It was hard work. When you worked those odd hours, and when you have little ones at home, it's hard to go home and sleep a couple hours and then get up and take care of the kids.

Wilma Woo and her husband, Danny, operated the New Chinatown Café from about 1939 to 1974. In 1977, they opened and operated the Quong Tuck Restaurant, which continued through 1985.

Sam Yee owned and operated the Hong Kong Restaurant, one of the most popular restaurants in Chinatown, for 37 years. He was the first person to teach the lion dance in Chinatown and performed with the Luck Ngi Musical Club since 1939. Yee served as president of the Chong Wa Benevolent Association for over 15 years.

Sam Yee

Born May 5, 1919, Canton, Kwangtung Province, China
Died December 25, 1996, Seattle, Washington

I came to the United States in 1939. When I first came, I was detained at the immigration station for 30 days. I was interrogated in detail by the immigration officials. I did not want to enter the U.S. because I felt that I would be treated badly.

I first worked in a lottery store on King Street. I entered the business following my grandfather, who sponsored my journey to the U.S. At that time, I would say that one out of every 10 Chinese worked in the lottery business. I remember that most of the Chinese I met were over 60 years old. I was among the youngest.

I stayed in Seattle for only eight months and I returned to Hong Kong by saving $80. I did not like the U.S., and when I arrived in Honolulu, I sent a letter back to my grandfather, telling him that after I got back to Hong Kong, I would never return to America. Ironically, when I arrived in Hong Kong, the Japanese began to occupy the colony and I had to come back to Seattle.

I went back to work for the lottery for $20 a month. An American man won the lottery and he was kind enough to give me 50 cents. I used the money to bet on the lottery and got very lucky by winning $2,000. With this money, I got out of the lottery business and bought a bar in Chinatown for $1,000. I operated this bar as a business even though I did not know English.

After six months, I was drafted for the War, but I heard that if I became a farmer, I would not have to go to war. Therefore, I went to Kent, Washington, and became a farmer and was able to avoid having to enlist in the military. Afterward, I also worked as a dry cleaner and operated a grocery store, selling rice.

I saved up money slowly through the years, and in 1947, I opened the Hong Kong Restaurant as a coffee shop. I built up the Hong Kong Restaurant from scratch and with very little resources. I operated the restaurant until 1984 when I sold it for a substantial sum.

In the old days, most of the Chinese worked in the hand laundries and restaurants. A few in grocery stores. There was nothing else to do. I went to Pacific School for only 26 days. My grandfather thought I should work for a living, rather than going to school. I learned English by just talking with Americans. My grandfather also taught me English through phonetic approximation of Toisan.

My first involvement with community organizations was with the Luck Ngi Musical Club in 1939. The club was started by a Mr. Louie in 1938 at the location where Barclay Seafood is located today. It was a group of young amateurs coming together to play Chinese music. I helped move the organization to its present location. It is a charitable organization. For the past two years, we performed to raise funds for the Kin On Nursing Home.

The new immigrants are more fortunate than the old immigrants. In the old days, there were no social services and welfare to help the poor. We did not know what to ask for. Nine out of 10 immigrants suffered in the old days. I could not even afford a watch. At most, my grandfather earned $60 a month. Today, there is more help and opportunities for the newcomers. I think it is good for the community.

I want to see a place opened up in Chinatown for the retirees to stop by and have tea and coffee and have a chance to talk about life, history and the future. People would be able to eat and drink and chat as long as they wished. This would be something like a social teahouse.

Gregory Chew came to Seattle to join his father, Chew Quay Fong, a cannery worker who lived in Chinatown. Chew worked as a waiter at the Hong Kong Restaurant for 32 years, retiring in 1984.

Gregory H. Chew

Born September 5, 1916, Fow Sek Village, Toisan District, Kwangtung Province, China
Died April 23, 1996, Seattle, Washington

I was born on September fifth, 1916, in Fow Sek Village in the province of Kwangtung. That's the American date. The village has a population of approximately 10,000. In fact, it's one of the largest villages in the Toisan area. I completed grade school and junior high in the village. Most of the other smaller villages didn't have their own school. We did.

It's September, 1930 when I arrived in this country. I came on the President Taft steamship with my brother, Hung Hong. The trip took 20 days. The first thing I remember when I landed was the Smith Tower, which was the tallest building at the time, 42 stories.

They detained me at the immigration station at First and Union until my hearing. It took about three weeks before my turn comes up. I didn't speak a word of English. At the immigration, they had an interpreter, and they ask about where you were born, which village, the size of the village and the population, and all your neighbors that's closest to you and also how big their families are and how many children they have. The only way they can tell if you are telling the truth is comparing your answer with the person who is the witness for you or comparing it with a brother or sister if they came before you. My brothers were witnesses for me. If they are satisfied with your answers, they issue you an I.C. – that's short for an identification certificate.

I started my laundry on Third Avenue and Seneca around 1935. My laundry was called the Continental Hand Laundry. My brother, Hung Hong, also worked there. It doesn't take too much capital to start a hand laundry. You don't need much equipment to start up. All you need is the irons, ironing table and shelving, which is just like a bookcase, so you can stack up the laundry. That's all.

Actually, we just do the finishing work at the hand laundry. When the customer brings in the soiled laundry, we record the order, sort it and mark a number or letter on the laundry with a pen – you use indelible ink – on the collar band. Then we send it out to a commercial laundry for the washing. After we get it back, we do the ironing, starching and all the finishing touches. Then we sort it out and repackage it. Normally, when we take in the laundry, it takes about four to five days before the customer picks it up. My customers were from the hotels in the area. Back then, there were a lot of hotels around there. It was 15 cents a shirt, and you cut it down – two for 25 cents – give the customer a bargain, special rate.

I started working as a waiter at the Hong Kong Restaurant in 1952. The thing I like about the job is I get to know so many people and talk to so many customers. The dislike of the job is the long hours, but that's their working hours, so you have to accept that. At that time, the jobs aren't that many to be had, so therefore, my thinking is: "You make a living."

I generally know most of the customers by name. Normally, some of the waiters, they don't care. I talk to the customers a lot and I communicate and try to help them order the different dishes. They appreciate that, and therefore, normally speaking, I think they tip me a little more than the other waiters.

The people, they walk in there and they say, "Where's Greg? I want him to come over here and help me with the menu." So that's how it kept me busy all the time. They like me to take care of the dinner for them.

In his younger years, Alfred Mar worked in his father's restaurants, including the Mar Café, which opened in 1927. During World War II, he bought a grocery store from a Japanese American family who was forced to leave Seattle. He operated the store, Mar's Grocery, until the early 1950s, when he sold the store and went to work as a meat cutter.

Alfred C. Mar

Born September 3, 1914, Seattle, Washington

When I was old enough, around 14 or 15, during school vacation, you would go down and meet the trains. They came in, one at eight and one at 8:30 in the morning, and you would see if there are any Chinese on the train. Then you would ask them where they are going or whether they care to come to your store and let us take care of them. My father was the Chinese passenger agent for Chicago-Milwaukee Railroad and American Mail Line. He also did a lot of salmon cannery contracting for labor. He had the store, Quong On, at 660 King Street.

When these people came to your store, the upstairs would be partitioned off and there would be two or three beds there. You had a person cook two meals a day for them. We had a truck and we would go down to the depot to get their baggage, or if they were leaving Seattle, you check their baggage for them at the depot. You would charge them so much a bag and so much for their meals and that was how you made your money. The Blue Funnel Line was handled by Yick Fung, Jimmy Mar's father's, and the Canadian Pacific was represented by Yee Chong, Hong Chin's father.

I went to grammar school at Leschi, right off Yesler and 32nd. I finished Garfield in three years, on the honor society all the time, but I didn't go to the University. The older brother went, but I didn't feel at the time that it was necessary. You could see quite a few Chinese that went to the University, but they still couldn't get decent jobs. In the olden days, you didn't have any protection. If some guys don't want to hire you because you're a Chinaman, so what? But as the minorities grew and as you got more Blacks in the surrounding area, that changed. Some of these things that the Blacks have pushed have benefited us as minorities, too. Otherwise it would still be "Ching, Ching Chinaman."

When we used to have the restaurant, every so often some of these younger Caucasians in their early 20s or so would come down and eat and dance and try to slip out. If there's a party of four, maybe two would slip out, and the others would try to slip out later, so you had to watch. They would try to take advantage of you because you were Chinese. It's changed a lot – what abuse we used to take, and what you younger ones don't have to take.

Back when I first went out to work for the American people in their businesses, it's 10:30 and they say, "Hey, come on. Let's go. Coffee break." You never had a coffee break when you had your own business. You worked. Lunchtime, you take a whole hour off for lunch, and you didn't really know what to do with yourself half of the time. It doesn't take you an hour to eat. And then at 2:30 or so, "Hey, come on. Let's go. Coffee break."

It was just strange to you when you yourself have worked many times seven days a week, 12 hours a day, and then you go out to work, you think, "God, look what I've missed all these years." In the olden days, you had to really knuckle down and work.

Mary Woo

Born October, 1916, Nanaimo, British Columbia

My husband came over from China in 1937. During that time, it was the Depression, and there's not much opportunity for newcomers from China. He associated with the Chong Wa Association, and he helps around there. Eventually, he went over to Charlie Wah's Wing Quong. Wing Quong was an herbal shop. John was an herb doctor there, and he helps quite a lot of people, even if you don't have money to pay for the herbs. He would write out prescriptions for the people coming into the Wing Quong Company. If they had money, they paid for the herbs and took them home to prepare later. If they couldn't afford the herbs, John would help. Wing Quong would pay for the herbs, and John wouldn't charge them. Lots of times, they would boil the herbs at Wing Quong for the individuals who lived in the small hotel rooms. These people didn't have any space to prepare the herbs. People were very thankful. They remember.

At the same time, in the evening, he would go over to Chong Wa and play the role of different characters in the opera to raise money for China at the time. The money they raised they used to aid the refugees in China. You've never seen a Chinese opera? How would I describe it? The costumes are beautiful. Each character would have their different costumes. If he's a warrior, he wears a warrior's costume. If he's a student, he wears what students wear. The girl – if she's a servant – she wears a different type. If it's one of these girls growing up in rich families, she would wear something different, much more elaborate. Every character, you can tell the difference by the way they perform.

We got married in July of '48, and then in '49, we opened the shop – Flowerland Florist. We had both Chinese and non-Chinese business. At the University of Washington, there were prom dances. We take orders for a lot of corsages and for other occasions. In the florist business, you have to work day and night, sometimes without stopping, even for coffee, because if you have weddings or funerals and other orders, you have to get them all ready for the next day's delivery.

Mary Woo was born in Canada, married her husband, John, and together they opened the Flowerland Florist. Her husband was a member of the Luck Ngi Musical Club and also an herbal doctor.

胡李卉蘭

Chong Wing Mar

Born November 2, 1923, Seung Gaung How Village, Toisan District, Kwangtung Province, China
Died 1996, Seattle, Washington

I started going to Chinatown when I find a job down there in one of the restaurants. Not waiter because I didn't know enough English at that time. I helped wash dishes and bus dishes. It wasn't a permanent job. It's just on weekends when you're going to school and you don't have the time to work every day.

When I worked in that gambling place, the biggest thing is that you got to have a strong will because otherwise you get contaminated. You see other people gambling in there. Making money is so easy. So you are tempted. You stay with those people every day. All they care about is gambling. You see what's going on. At that age – you're only 20 or 21 – you start to make up your mind, "I don't want any part of it." The only thing you care about is to finish your job and do other things.

So I said I want to go back to school and I saw the G.I. Bill, so I started going to school. At first, I couldn't get into any university because I didn't have a high school diploma. So I came back to finish high school at Broadway. I finished it – it was supposed to be three years of high school – in one year. I was pretty good at that time. At that age, you're a lot smarter than when you're older. When I finished that, I entered the University of Washington.

Chong Wing Mar came over to America in 1938. Drafted into World War II and placed in the 14th Air Service Group who maintained the Flying Tigers, Mar later used his G.I. Bill to fulfill a degree in electrical engineering. He retired in 1984. Mar loved to play tennis.

Lohman Jang

Born November 28, 1922, Hong Kong
Died June 24, 2001, Seattle, Washington

In the old days, we were called butchers. Nowadays, the correct term is meat cutters. I was in the meat cutting business for over 40 years.

In those days, a steak cost approximately $1.59 a pound. Nowadays, it costs $4 to $5 a pound. Customers often consulted with me on the preparation of the meats because I had the reputation of being an excellent cook. I was very particular about how I cut the meat, making sure I followed U.S. Department of Agriculture standards.

My apprenticeship started with Al Mar's grocery on 12th and Yesler. Then I had my own grocery store on 14th and Yesler. From there, I went to Albertson's and Safeway. I finally had a partnership at Russell's Meat Market in Chinatown.

I enjoyed Russell's the most because it was in Chinatown and I could talk to the customers in Chinese. I felt at home there.

Lohman Jang was still living in Hong Kong during the bombing of Pearl Harbor. He later joined the U.S. Navy, which deployed him to Japan where he witnessed the signing of the peace treaty.

May G. Woo

Born July 8, 1896, Seattle, Washington
Died January 11, 1995, Canton, Kwangtung Province, China

My mother came from Kwangtung Province. She was brought to Seattle by a relative. According to my half-sister, Father had four wives. The first one died a short time after she came to our village. The second one bore Father one son and two daughters. The son was not a successful man. Father was displeased with him because he failed in every business he did. As the second wife did not like to go to America, Father married a third woman, but she left our village secretly. So Father looked for a fourth woman. She was the mother of all the children born in Seattle. She bore Father nine children, five daughters and four sons. Now, only three are living. She came to Hong Kong in 1933, but returned to Seattle after staying in Hong Kong for a year. She liked America better. She died in 1963.

I was enrolled at the University of Washington in 1917. I graduated in 1921. I could get a college education because I am the oldest girl in the family. Margaret Chin, granddaughter of Chin Gee Hee, a Chinese pioneer, was the first Chinese girl to study at the University, but she did not graduate because she studied only one or two years. I was the first Chinese girl to graduate from the University.

I studied education. I also am the only girl in my family who has a knowledge of Chinese. I studied Chinese whenever I had a chance. All my sisters had no patience to study it. I left Seattle with my husband in October or November, 1921. I went to China to teach English because it was my ambition to do so.

I was forced to marry because of the tradition of Toisan people that girls should get married. My father introduced me to a man. I do not use my married name because I had an unhappy married life.

May Woo was the first Chinese woman to graduate from the University of Washington. She earned a bachelor's degree in education in 1921. She last lived in Canton, China and taught in Chinese middle schools for 30 years.

Mary Doung Chinn

Born March 30, 1913, Seattle, Washington
Died March 30, 2000, Seattle, Washington

In our family, we had such a big family and just one salary. My dad was working and just one salary, there's no way you could send the girls to college. There were three girls in the family. None of us had the opportunity to go. The boys would work during the summer in the canneries and save their money to go. I think of my five brothers, just one went to college. It's not like today – you can get scholarships, which is good.

I think I Magnin's was the first one to hire Chinese girls to work there. In those days, if you had a job, you also had to do maid duties on the side. They'd expect me to do maid work like cleaning mirrors. At the Fifth Avenue Theatre, I did ushering in the lounges and I worked in the checkroom. I had to do maid work in the ladies room. Fortunately, if you come across a good boss, you overlook those things. But the climate was like that. I remember they wouldn't allow us to join the union even though all the usherettes belonged. But later on, after the War, they let us join.

In those days, we didn't have the opportunity like the young folks have today. If you got a good job, you were not allowed to progress on your ability because of racist problems.

Mary Doung Chinn worked for the federal government for 22 years as a secretary and a claims examiner. She retired in 1974.

陳曾玉英

Jeni Kay Fung worked for 25 years at the University of Washington, spending her last 12 years as Assistant to the Dean of the School of Nursing. Since her retirement in 1988, she has devoted countless hours to assisting in publicity and fundraising efforts for the Kin On Nursing Home, the only bilingual Chinese nursing home in the Pacific Northwest.

馮駱月仙

Jeni Kay Fung

Born January 6, 1925, Olympia, Washington

My mother was a tiny woman, under five feet tall. Before she was married, she had her feet bound. When she was married, my father's family told her to unbind her feet. By then, they were already so deformed and so terrible, so she lived the rest of her life with semi-bound feet. That probably caused her more consternation than anything else – the pain and the discomfort that came from that. Up to the 1930s, her primary job was to bring up the children, which must have been rather difficult for someone who had semi-bound feet and did not speak English. There must have been a terrible lack of freedom for women of that generation.

Remarkably, she was able to do more work than anybody I could ever think of. She was a very, very hard worker. She was on her feet all the time. Her goal was to make sure that the family survived. In the heart of the Depression, my father had to work in a variety of establishments – including a restaurant in Seattle called the Hankow Café on Jackson Street. She felt kind of helpless, being in Olympia and not being able to do well with the family, so she decided that she was going to open a restaurant all on her own – with the help of three kids, three of us. My sister and my brother and myself were the only ones left in the family at that time. The older ones had married and gone away. She said that if we opened the restaurant and we took a storefront and if we could do $20 worth of business a day and feed ourselves, we could do okay – we could make out. This was our own family restaurant called Kay's Café, in Olympia. It was opened in 1940.

When you think of the Depression, for many families, I don't think college was a real goal. We never broached the subject, and my parents, having no formal education, never sought to have us look beyond. My father had, I think, two years of grade school, and my brother, Henry, may have gone only to grade school. None of my other brothers and sisters went to college after they graduated from high school.

I had a goal for myself very early on that I wanted to go to college. I knew that I wanted to do more with my life than just high school. So we had a big running argument for about two years – between myself and my parents – about whether I could go to college. They certainly felt that it was not necessary. And so I made a pledge to myself when I was in high school. I did my work at the restaurant as a waitress, but I also worked in a dress shop right after school before the restaurant opened and on Saturdays and Sundays in the daytime, and made enough money to pay two years of tuition at the University of Washington. I defied my parents' wishes and sent in the applications and forms for a dormitory. It came through and I was accepted. So in the fall of '45, I decided I was going to move to Seattle to enter the University of Washington. And my father relented that last week and my mother finally agreed.

I remember saying to my mother, when I was in despair at raising children, "How do I know I'm doing a good job? I'm not trained to do this! Nobody's ever told me how to do this!" And she said, "You won't know until your kids are 40 and they have families of their own, so don't worry about it."

I thought that was a very sage comment from her because now my kids are not quite 40 yet, but they have their own families, and I'm seeing how they're raising their children and I'm saying, "Hey, we didn't do such a bad job after all!" I think we succeeded. So I think the best time of my life is now.

David H. Woo

Born April 7, 1912, Seattle, Washington
Died April 23, 1992, Seattle, Washington

I volunteered for the Coast Guard. They took me in and asked me what tribe I belonged to. I said, "I don't belong to any tribe. I'm Chinese." "Oh," they said. "We can't take you." I said, "Why?" "Because we have to have an affidavit from certain respectable people saying that you're a person of good respect and dependable and all of that." So I went out and got the head of immigration, who was my father's friend, and he wrote out that I'm from a good family and all that. And I went to another guy, a white guy – it all has to be white guys – I got three, and by then, they accepted me. It's the first time I was in the air corps.

They take Chinese volunteers, but only for the mess hall. They will draft you and put you in the kitchen, but they won't take Chinese for any other department of the Navy.

I was involved in the first mission over German Proper. I was on the plane that pioneered that. I was assistant radio operator and

gunner. Over Dunkirk, we were looking for a Japanese ship that we were going to bomb. We hit it, and on the way out, they hit us, and so we went down. We got blown out. I pulled ripcord and came down, and they were shooting at me with tracers. I didn't get hit, but I shattered my ankle on landing.

The Germans sent me off to camp – interrogation camp. A little dungeon. There was no air or nothing. They asked me where I was from, what race I was, and what nationality I was. I always said, "I'm American." And they said, "You're not American. You're something else." They slapped me. Well, they kept asking and asking, then they gave up and let me out where the other prisoners are. So from there, I was sent to the prison camp.

I was in Stalag 17, in what they called the Whitehouse. I was in charge of the mail – coming in and going out. I was also co-editor of the underground news. One guy that speaks German – he's a Jew named Frank Ottinger – he and I get together every day and write up the news sheet. And as soon as the Germans are gone and the lights are out, we get somebody to go around and read the news stories off. We would make up most of it – morale builders.

One night, the Germans started chasing us out of the camp. They were telling us, "The Russians are coming. They're shelling Vienna. Pack your things and we're moving out." So we got a bunch of dogs and our tracers out and we kept walking. That was really pretty terrible. We would sleep in the snow – the rain and the snow. We got soaking wet all the time. Fortunately, I had a couple of good buddies that took care of me. They carried my pack and they made me sleep in the middle, while they slept one on either side of me – to keep me warm.

Well, on that forced march, we were walking one night, we heard a lot of gunfire. The Americans had contacted the Germans. It took two or three weeks before the Americans caught up with us. They were fighting it out right on the Inns River, and so we knew General Patton's troops were over there. The Germans surrendered to the Americans, and finally, an American captain came in and said, "Gentlemen, you are free." When that captain came to tell us we're free, everybody cried.

When I was in the prison camp, I had thought, when I get back, I'll do two things. I'm going to the gambling house and I'm going to gamble one $1,000 hand with my back pay. I said to myself, "I'm going to double my money right there." And the second thing I'll do, I think I'll organize a veterans group because I know all of my friends were in the service, practically all of them. So I did both.

David Hong Woo, best known to his friends as "Gobby," was an aerial gunner pilot on a B-24 mission over Germany during World War II. He survived 27 months of confinement in German prison camps, including Stalag 17B, the Austrian camp immortalized in a film starring William Holden. He returned to Seattle and founded a Chinese American veterans' group, the Cathay Post #186 of the American Legion.

James Locke

Born October 15, 1917, Git Loong Village, Toisan District, Kwangtung Province, China

The Chinese people are the contractors for the cannery, right? They do the hiring, so mostly all Chinese and Filipinos. They came up from California every year. Then when the cannery season's over, when we came back, then they go back to California to work in the farm again or somewhere.

Summertime you go. Mostly go up in June after school's out, go up there and earn some money. You only work about a month and a half. Not quite two months. You eat there in the bunk houses, Chinese food, not very good, but salmon every day. Mostly all Chinese people up there, too. All Chinese school kids and older men. Mostly all work in the dry warehouse. Get the boxes and then put the canned salmon into the case. I was working in the fish house. I don't know how come they put me in the fish house. Upstairs in the fish house, they put the can with the bottom on, see? Come through the line, and then they put the salmon in the can, and then the people sit there and see if anything wrong with the fish. Sometimes they might have to turn it or cut off something. I was the one that when the canned salmon comes through the line you put some caps on the machine to cap the salmon. Put the lid on the machine, and then goes down the line and goes into cases of it. Then they go into a steamer.

I was drafted before Pearl Harbor in 1940. When you're drafted, you have to tell what you do. I said I'm a cook, so they put me in the kitchen. We facing combat, but not like the frontline. We were sent to the service company, carry ammunition, gasoline and foodstuff to the frontline. We went to England for the invasion, right down by the coast between England and France. I was the mess sergeant in charge of officers' mess. We eat good, I'll tell you that! Steak all the time. We took over the hotel there. Fancy hotel, they got broilers, so we have broiled steak, pork chops. Then I have to make three kinds of ice cream every night. Take it up to an English ice cream parlor and freeze it for the next day's dessert.

In those days, there's no combat yet. It's still before D-Day. At nighttime, usually there's German V-bomb, you know? They come all over the place. Boy, when they come, when you hear the noise, it's okay. But once you don't hear the noise, you better go down to the basement because that's when they gonna' drop then. They hit us pretty good, but didn't hit the hotel.

During the German offensive there, we almost got blown out of the hilltop. All our supplies was on top of the mountain there. Evidently, the Germans had captured one of our spotter planes. So we thought it was our own plane, but it was a German plane, so they were able to direct all the artillery right on top of us. We had to get the heck out of there in a hurry. Some of the ammunition trucks got blown up and some of the gasoline truck was blown up. One more time, too, was when we were delivering ammunition and gasoline to the frontline. We were stopping there on the side of the road and we almost got caught off there, too. A few soldiers got killed, but it wasn't as bad as we thought. So there's two close calls that we had.

James Locke's father was the head chef at Virginia Mason Hospital. Locke later owned a restaurant with friends and then a grocery store from 1960 to 1980. Locke also helped his son, Gary, campaign successfully for many positions in government, including King County Executive and Washington State Governor. Locke and his wife, Julie, have five children.

駱榮碩

Bill Lee

Born August 24, 1922, Toisan District, Kwangtung Province, China

My dad brought me to America when I was 13 years old. We went to Hamilton, Montana, where my dad and uncle had a restaurant for many years. When I first came to this country, I didn't speak a word of English, so I was enrolled in the first grade. In the first year, I attended first, second and third grades. By progressing at about that speed, I eventually graduated high school when I was 20 years old.

I didn't have any problems in school during my first year because I didn't understand what was said about me. I tried and avoided trouble at any cost. Being a 13-year-old immigrant, I had a few fights in school because some boys were teasing me, such as "Chinky Chinky Chinaman," but I had more friends than enemies in school.

Growing up, Bill Lee always enjoyed working on engines and fixing broken appliances. He even developed a motor for his bicycle. As an adult, he became a civil engineer for the Washington State Highway Department where he was involved in the design of I-90 and I-5. He later worked on Sea Tac Airport's runway and terminal expansion to fit the large size of the Boeing Company's 747 aircraft.

I learned most of my English from a customer in our restaurant. His name was Mr. Hops. After dinner each day, he would spend about a half to one hour with me on reading. By the time I was a 16-year-old fifth grader, I was completely Americanized and began to gain much respect from all of my classmates.

I was not there when high school graduation took place. World War II was going on and I was about to be drafted. At that time, I was weighing about 120 pounds. I came to the conclusion that I would come out second best in hand-to-hand combat, so I decided that I should strengthen my brain power in order to have a better chance to survive the war. I found out there was a school in Helena that teaches radio communication. The school was called NYA – National Youth Authority. While attending this school, we were provided with board and room and a little spending money. The training was quite intense. The instructors would not accept any nonsense at all. It's all business all day long. We practiced mostly on the receiving and sending of Morse code messages, and in between, we learned radio repair work and theory. It was the best thing that I ever did in my life.

Just before the class was done, I notified my draft board that I would be available for army service. They did not waste any time. The next thing I knew I was in the army. I was scared half to death for being in the army and in an entirely different environment. Even more surprise, I found myself assigned to a heavy weapons company, which specialized in handling machine guns of all kinds – mortars, bazookas and so on. I said to myself, "Hey, this was not for me." Within a week, I found the radio communication training company in camp, went over there and told them that I just had training in radio communication. The sergeant said, "Well, let's go find out." He took me into a school room and turned on the code machine and said, "Show me what you can do." I was more nervous than the cat on a hot tin roof, but I took and sent the messages for the sergeant as best as I could. Within a matter of a few days, the sergeant had me transferred to his company.

Shortly after I arrived in Italy, I was assigned to a very special unit. A small group of men in a company called SIAM, Signal Information and Monitoring Service. Our assignment was gathering up all the battle information from the frontline and passing them on to the generals and colonels for action. We had to move frequently and on very short notice at times because the enemy would listen and zero in on our radio signals. The Germans tried everything to wipe us out, so we don't stay in one place very long. That was how we kept from being killed.

Eventually, the Allied Commanders decided that the Seventh Army would be the one to make the invasion from South France. My unit was with General Mark Clark's Fifth Army fighting near Rome, Italy, at the time when the invasion decision was made. General Eisenhower took us away from General Mark Clark and assigned us to the Seventh Army for the southern France invasion, which we did.

Whenever the enemy planes came, the sky would be red, filled with tracers like our Fourth of July celebrations. It was a scary time whenever this happened. Everybody's nerves was shot most of the time. You just don't believe how scared one can be under those circumstances, especially the feeling of being killed at any moment. I carried a pistol and carbine 24 hours a day – my security blanket. I was not about to give up my life without a good fight. I cleaned and oiled these weapons once a day. They were the only insurance policies that I had.

Eugene Ko's father was a cannery foreman in Alaska. His mother was a housewife who worked as a Boeing riveter during World War II. When Ko started his medical practice in 1956, he was one of only three Chinese physicians in Seattle. He has served many Asian families on Beacon Hill.

Eugene Ko

Born March 23, 1926, Seattle, Washington

In the summer when the War first started, in 1941, there weren't very many able-bodied men around, so a group of us high school kids were recruited from Seattle to go to Astoria, Oregon to work in the canneries. We did the hardest jobs. We were gang knifers. People who cleaned the fish would send it down to us, throw it into a big slot. There was a big guillotine that had 20 blades in it. Hoonk! You cut the whole fish into slices, put the slices in a box and send it down the line to the women who put them in cans. They fit them in the cans and send it down. A top would be put on it.

I was 130 pounds, 16 years old. It was hard work. During the run, we worked 16, 17 hours a day. We were contract laborers. The Wong family contracted for us to be paid so much a season. They fed us and we slept in a bunkhouse. For breakfast, lunch and dinner, you came in and sat at your own table, six to eight people. They bring in a pot of rice and a dish or two. The contractor, the less money he put into food, the more he pockets. That's why that system was so bad. He was motivated not to treat you very well or put out very much in the way of expenses. They made money on those people. Man's inhumanity to man. But that was dog eat dog in those days. That's the way the game was played.

When I was 18, I was drafted into the service. I went into the Navy. They give you a series of aptitude tests, so if your grades are up a little bit, you get a choice of what sub-branch you want to be in – gunnery mate, cook, pharmacist's mate. I chose pharmacist's mate because I was semi-interested in what the medicine game was like. So after three months in boot camp, I went to the hospital corps school for three months and then I went to the hospitals to work. Fortunately, I didn't go overseas.

I got a chance to be the lowest person on the totem pole as far as medicine was concerned. Made beds, carried bed pans, scrubbed floors. Every evening, when we were on cleanup detail, we'd stand 15 across and the person who was over us inspected our nails to make sure they were clean. Then we went around buffing and scrubbing the floors. Working with patients and doing the most menial jobs made me realize there was a great separation between the ordinary workers in the hospitals and the doctors and nurses. Their responsibilities were great and they did some very spectacular things, meaningful things. And then I come in and mop up. I realized I didn't want to be on that end. So when I was released from the service, after a couple of years, I went back to the UW [University of Washington].

At that time, the medical school was new. I was in the fourth class. There's an unwritten quota at that time. There could only be two Asians in each class. So there was Haruto Sekijima and I in the class. I think one of the key things I told them was what my plan was – to open a clinic in Chinatown. A doctor to people that I knew, since I grew up in this community. No one knew many people that knew the language, so they thought that was a plus.

Dr. Ernest Ching was on Sixth and Jackson, and Dr. Henry Luke was in Chinatown, on Eighth Avenue, towards Weller. They were fairly well established, so I went to Beacon Hill where Chinese families were moving. That was in 1956. I think being a doctor provides a very good life. Not just economically, but a feeling that you're doing something good for people. It's been very satisfying. This is my 36th year. Slowly I'm going to retire – if I can get someone to take over mainly the older patients, the older Chinese patients. There are a lot of older Chinese who are dependent on me. Maybe I think they are dependent on me. They could easily transfer – there's half a dozen Chinese doctors – but there's a certain loyalty that's built in.

Richard Lew Kay is the son of Lew G. Kay, the first Chinese to graduate from the University of Washington in 1909, and the grandson of Goon Dip, one of the most prominent Chinese merchants in the Northwest. Kay was a pharmacist on Beacon Hill from 1959 to 1997. He now works part-time as a relief pharmacist for King County.

Richard Lew Kay

Born January 10, 1929, Seattle, Washington

For some reason, my mother didn't want to enroll me in Chinese school down in Chinatown. She didn't drive, so it might have been a problem getting me down, unless I walked, and she didn't want me to walk. So she brought these tutors up. They would finish with their regular classes, then come up and give me about an hour, three times a week. She did this for about three or four years. Finally, they found out how thick-skulled I was and gave up. My mom said, "I don't know if he's learning too much." I learned to write my name, that's about all. I didn't get to run around with my friends at Chinese school and drop water balloons from the second floor. I guess my mother heard about these things, so she didn't want me to go.

I used to wear the China button – red, white and blue. I would stand at a bus stop and wait for a bus. The bus driver would look at me and see the China button and let me in. There were the Japanese people standing at the bus stop with me, and they wouldn't even let them in without the button. Some of my Japanese friends asked me if they could borrow the button when they went downtown. I said, "Sure." So my Japanese friends wore the button.

I remember my dad wouldn't want me to play with the Japanese boys. It affected him and the older Chinese people at the time. They felt more strongly against mingling with Japanese people. I didn't mind. We would still play even if parents didn't know about it. After the war ended, it got better. The older Chinese, it took longer to adjust – especially if they had relatives in China who died at the hands of the Japanese. Time heals things. It's like a little Hawaii here, with Japanese marrying Chinese.

During the time I was in school, the Korean War broke out about 1950. I was called into active service in the Army. I spent one year in the States, then I went to Korea for one year. While in Korea, I was assigned to a Quartermaster, and we did a lot of work in supplies and services for the frontline soldiers. We were more in the backlines with supplies, food, clothing and civilian type services such as running bakeries, laundries, identifying indigenous Korean labor pool and working in hospitals.

Sometimes the Caucasian soldiers would mix me up. At a distance, they would glance at me and think I was Korean. They would say, "Hey, boy! Come over here and help me do this." And when I came close, they found out I was a Lieutenant in the Army, and they would say, "Oh, I'm sorry, sir." They would apologize right away. It made me laugh at them. I didn't mind it too much. But some of the Caucasians looked down on the Koreans there.

The Koreans enjoyed having me around. They thought I was one of them. It was so funny, a Chinese in the American Army. They would say, "Chinese – same, same," and I would say, "Chinese, yeah, same, same – but not really same, same." I would say I'm American Chinese and try to make the difference. But I had a lot of fun with them.

I was attached to the hospital, helping the hospital people with the Army problems and the personnel problems. I got interested in the pharmacy. After I came back from the Army in '53, I enrolled in the UW [University of Washington] in pharmacy. I used the G.I. Bill to help get me through school, and I went through pharmacy in three years. After that, I went to work for G.O. Guy Drugstore chain. After two years, I started my own pharmacy on Beacon Hill in 1959. I've been on the Hill for 35 years.

Hen Sen Chin

Born June 23, 1923, Toisan District, Kwangtung Province, China

I was born in China, in the village. After I was born, my father came back to work in Bellingham. He cooked for some American family. When I was three years old, my mother told me that he was dead. This meant when I was young, I only had my mother to support me.

I have three brothers. I am the youngest. I have one sister, the oldest, but she was an adopted sister. When they are big enough, they all come back to America. I come three times, back and forth. When I was 10 years old, then I come over here. After a year and a half, I go back because they want me to go to school in China. My mom want me there because my mom was the only one by herself.

In China, only one year in high school. At that time, the Second World War, Japanese hit. The first time Japanese airplane bombed Toisan, everybody scared. Right away I go back to the village. I was 13. I did not stay too long in the village. Right away I go back

to America. I went to Pacific School on 12th Avenue with all the foreign class: Chinese, Japanese, even European. Only English classes.

I was there about a year and a half and then I really made up my mind to learn herbs. I go back to Hong Kong. I had a friend who opened a rice store. He know my teacher in the school, a special school just for herbs, to learn herb and later on learn to be an herb doctor. Generally, people learn in about five years. I was about 15 or 17 and stayed there until about I was 22 or 23 years old.

When I graduated, the Japanese fight Hong Kong, so right away I go back to the village. I was a doctor already, but at that time only one sickness – hunger. No food, no job, nothing you can do. Many people died of hunger in the village. Even if someone die in the house, nobody know, because when you are hungry, you cannot walk, cannot go out. To be a good doctor, very easy if you can buy hundreds and hundreds pound of rice. Then, people have no sickness.

At the end of World War II, Hen Sen Chin came back to America to practice herbal medicine. He washed dishes in a Chinese restaurant in Seattle, saved his money, then went to work as an herbalist in San Francisco and New York. In 1950, he returned to Seattle to start his own herb shop in Chinatown.

After Second World War ended, we go back to Hong Kong. Right away I register to get a boat to come back to America. In 1950, I started the herb store at the corner of King and Eighth in Seattle. It was very hard because not too many people believe in it. Even Chinese people, because no herb store in Seattle for a long time. Seattle town small and too long no herb doctor here, so people forgot it. Although I start with few patients, slowly get better and better. Main thing I believe is when you help the patient, the patient help you. I was there 40 years.

What does it mean to be a doctor? To us, if a doctor help the patient, then good doctor. If only talk but still no help, then, no matter what, even if patient believe in the beginning, they will not stay too long. Chinese herb help, American drug help, but no matter what, if not right drug, if not right herb, not help. Many Westerners think if they have a fever and treat fever so it go down, then everything all right. But sometimes not. Really good doctor, they find out. We have another rule like this: before you help the case, you do not know the case. If you don't help the case, then how do you know what it is?

To take care of your own health, first take care of your condition – this means living good, peace with yourself. The main thing is you are peaceful. Second, keep on good diet. Third, watch the changing weather. You don't want to catch cold. Even from long, long time ago, get a long life if follow this.

Frank Chong, the son of cannery contractor Chong Lock, worked as a journeyman shipfitter at the Bremerton shipyards during World War II. He was later recruited by the U.S. Navy to work as a quality control inspector at the Lockheed Shipbuilding Company in Seattle. He retired from government service in 1978.

Frank L. Chong

Born September 29, 1912, Portland, Oregon

When we were in high school, we'd go to the theater – two or three of us. They had ushers there. They stand right at the entrance of the seating area. You come in – they take one look at you, and if you're an Oriental or a Black, they routed you upstairs. And those were supposed to be the worst seats in the theater. They wouldn't let you sit downstairs. If you complain, you were a minority, just one person. They didn't pay any attention to you.

My interest was in gasoline engines. The Model T Ford was a very famous automobile in those days. Henry Ford built the first Model T in 1912 about the time I was born, and this Model T Ford was still in existence until 1930. I chose courses in automobile engines because that was the coming thing at the time.

After I graduated from automobile school, my dad says, "Maybe we'd better lease a garage and see what you can do with it." We leased a garage. I ran that garage for a couple years. Sorry to say I just ran it into the ground. Those things don't work out because of discrimination. When they see you're an Oriental, they don't want to patronize you.

I came to Seattle in 1942. I used to live on Seventh Avenue. I only had a little room. It had a bed and a washbasin. It's still there. I had to pay $10 a month for that room. Right underneath me was the Twin Dragon Café. And, boy, they had a dance floor and they had a jukebox! It used to be that all the riffraff goes in down there – these sailors and their girlfriends – and they would sit there, probably dance all night. It was two or three o'clock in the morning before they would close down the jukebox.

During the War, I was working in the shipyard over in Bremerton. I commuted between Seattle and Bremerton. That was from 1941 until 1946. I had applied for a job at the Navy yard because they wouldn't hire us in Oregon. You're a minority and you're Oriental – they didn't hire anybody of that type. So we said, "Well, we can't get a job here. We might as well go to the government." We applied for the job and we got the job. That's how I wound up in Seattle.

After the War was over, they laid off a lot of people over there because they didn't need that type of help anymore. So in 1946, I applied for this job down here at the GMC Truck Center. They sent me a letter saying that they don't hire minorities. The only reason I applied was because they needed mechanics, and I was a mechanic. And, well, you saw the results.

Hong Y. Chin

Born September 15, 1909, Canton, Kwangtung Province, China
Died June 26, 1993, Seattle, Washington

One of the reasons I came over is because they tried to catch me for ransom. At that time, there was a lot of robbery, trying to hold Chinese for ransom and so forth. My father is here and they know they can extract money from me so I'm running and hiding. So he sent for us, my mother and myself. We came over in 1918.

My father, Chin Tan, was one of the few Chinese at that time who speak English. He learn his English in church – First Baptist Church up on Madison Street. He was an agent for Canadian Pacific Station Line and Northern Pacific Railroad Line. You know 99 out of 100 Chinese go by steerage, which is real rough. They stay in the bottom of the boat – no air, no nothing because it was more economical. They don't allow womenfolk to come over unless you're born here and there were very few born here. If you go back to China and get married, you cannot bring your wife over because you're not a citizen. They restrict them

After completing college at the University of Washington, Hong Chin enrolled at a U.S. Military School in Santa Maria, California. In 1932, he became one of the first Chinese Americans to receive a pilot's license. Later, he and his wife, Daisy, operated a grocery store on Beacon Hill and worked in real estate. Photo circa 1932.

from coming in because they're afraid the child born here will take away the jobs. So for many years, there was only about 2,000 Chinese in the whole city of Seattle. They only allow 100 Chinese a year to come to the United States. In England, they got thousands and thousands – they can come anytime they want to.

My father was supposed to be an American citizen. He was here before the San Francisco fire when all the Chinese claim they were born here. They can't prove it, they can't disprove it, either, so therefore, they let him bring my mother and me. I've heard the people here resent the Chinese. My dad told me one time they take him down to the dock and several Chinese were pushed down on the dock and drowned.

When I went to the University of Washington, I wanted to take architecture. At that time, Lindbergh flew to Paris and somehow, I'm crazy enough – I changed my major to aeronautics. That's in 1932. I think I was the first one in the Northwest. We used to fly formation in the Santa Maria area. I went to apply for ferrying planes between United States and Africa during World War II. I was married and I got two boys at the time. If I got killed, they have to support the whole family. They don't want that. They say you better go and work for the industry.

About five or six months after World War II, they were recruiting all people to work for Boeing. I went to apply. I went there four or five times, and they just throw my application in the waste basket. Only Caucasian people get a job right away. They wouldn't hire Chinese. I was so mad. I was afraid that if I go home, I take it out on my wife. So you know what I did? Before, they didn't have the floating bridge, so I drive around Renton and then go around Lake Washington. About two or three hours later, I go up to Kirkland and around the lake. When I cool off, I went home and my wife was mad at me because I didn't come home.

Just about two years after World War II, Frank Mar was the first Chinese they hire at Boeing. I could have probably got in after that. Maybe I was a little bit mad, but you could only go so far with Boeing. I wanted to work for myself, so I bought a grocery store up on 20th and Beacon Avenue. We worked there for about 20 years. We work 17 hours a day – don't have too much time with family.

I think we have lots better opportunities now than before. I think it is due to the Black people. They are more vocal than the Chinese. The Chinese are not enough – they should be more vocal, and then, they get all the things. Relative to getting a job and so forth, a lot prefer to hire the Chinese and Japanese than Black people. So what they fight for we get the benefit of.

Dorothy Chun

Born December 7, 1911, Hong Kong
Died July 14, 2003, Seattle, Washington

I want to tell you about my father. He's a very good father. He loves the family so much, and he loves the children so much. He hires the scholars, the private teachers, to teach the children. He thinks the Chinese have to be good in Chinese literature, so when we are kids, we write very good literature at home.

When we were very little, about eight to 12 years old, we want to go to school. We didn't tell my father. We just go to take a test, and the school tell my father our literature is very good, and my father is very happy to let us go to public school. He loved us so much!

My father said, "When you are young, you listen to your father. When you are married, you obey your husband. When you are old, you obey your son." I was married at 17. My marriage is by matchmaker. I never know my husband. We get engaged and get married, and the next year he bring me to America. I bring one servant to America, but in 1933, during that age, in America, there is a great shortage of women. When I come out, every man come out of the street to look at me. I feel bashful. I don't want to walk in Chinatown. There's no women. My servant come, and in six months, she got married. I got no more servant. I don't know how to do anything. I feel homesick all the time.

I was just coming to America during the Depression. We own lots of land and we own a building. We couldn't pay tax because of the Depression. We lost everything on my husband's side. That's why my husband have no money. That's why I start a business myself. I worked very hard. About 10, 11 hours. Six days. I don't know English, I don't work before, and I have no experience. I never make money in my life, and I told my father, "Don't send me any money." I want to be on my own. I don't want my father to support me. I want to do something myself.

My restaurant was named Shangri-la Café, downtown, at First and Seneca. I started it in 1942. The café seats 60 people, and mostly it's American people coming in to eat. No Chinese coming to eat. We served Chinese food like sweet and sour, fried rice, egg foo young, chow mein, chop suey. Once they come in, they always come back to eat, so it makes me feel just like they are a friend, not a customer.

At my location is all sailors and soldiers. My customers is workingmen. The jukebox always jammed up with quarters because they sit there all night to listen to the music. I got so much business, I don't know how to handle it. I got scared. I didn't tell my husband I'm afraid that I can't do it. But when I opened that day, I take him down there. It's so beautiful. I don't know why, but I just always want to be independent.

My customers all just like a family, treat me so good. I really enjoy it. One year, seamen's strike, they all poor, and I give them a meal ticket – five dollars each – and they eat. And after they ship out again and they are over the strike, they send me the money from other towns. Even now, I see them in Chinatown, and they say, "Dorothy! You fed me long time ago." I recognize some of them. I feel so happy all my life because I helped people. Now, I don't feel homesick. I like American ways, I live American way, so I turned out to be American. That's my home, and I've got everything.

After retiring, Dorothy Chun spent her lunchtime each weekday volunteering at a meal program serving the Asian elderly at the Bush Hotel in Chinatown. This volunteer work, which she loved, dovetailed her earlier career as owner and operator of a Chinese restaurant in downtown Seattle, from 1942 to the early 1960s.

Wai Eng

Born 1929, Toisan District, Kwangtung Province, China

I started the Kau Kau Restaurant on Second Avenue. When I first started, it was not a barbecue restaurant. It served Chinese lunch, dinner and cocktails. I worked from six o'clock in the morning until nine o'clock at night. Every day, I was there all the time, no matter what. Sixteen hours a day. I worked there from 1959 'til 1970. For 11 years, I didn't have a vacation. We got a lot of customers, but don't forget – we had a lot of heavy payments. My salary went to pay the loans. So we made a living, but we didn't have any money to go anywhere.

May, 1970 was my last payment. I felt the happiest moment of my life was after May. Because I felt from then on, that money goes to me where I can use it. In July, I took my whole family for a long vacation in Hong Kong.

In 1972, I bought that old Merry Meat Market. They sold meat and fish. It was vacant for three years. I didn't know what to do with it. Then finally, in 1974, my brother and I sat together and we talked about what we were going to do with this place. We

figured we didn't have any barbecue place in Chinatown for more than a quarter of a century, maybe we'll open a barbecue place.

I think one of the reasons is that from 1950 to 1970, there was no immigrant community. But after the Vietnam War, so many new immigrants came from Vietnam, and with more people coming in here, that's why these barbecue items became very popular for the Chinese and Vietnamese. That's why it's going very strong now.

We work very hard. Our barbecue pork is the best item there. It sells the most. Before, I sold a lot of duck. I sold maybe 30, 40, maybe up to 60 ducks a day. Now, the duck volume has come down, but the barbecue pork remains the same, even up a little more. Business is very interesting, very funny. You cannot figure it out.

In 1958, Wai Eng went downtown searching for a place to open a restaurant, anticipating the many people who would flood Seattle for the 1962 World's Fair. On borrowed money, he started the Kau Kau Restaurant. Later, he started another popular barbecue restaurant of the same name in Chinatown. He spearheaded the 1989 development of the Eng Suey Sun Plaza, a commercial development that provides a headquarters for the Seattle chapter of the Eng Association.

In 1977, I opened the Korean Ginseng Center. I was in the U.S. Army in Korea from 1951 to 1953, so I had a good friend in Korea. We found each other back in the early part of the 1970s. From then on, we built up a relationship. Ginseng is one of the most expensive food substances on Earth. Not very many people can afford to eat it everyday, but more and more people believe in ginseng. Most of my ginseng customers are American people. They take capsules, extracts, powders – the easy way to take it. Most Chinese people, they have to cook it for eight hours, so they drink the nectar from it. American people do not waste time to do all that, so all they do is pop a couple drops in their mouth and swallow it down.

The ginseng root itself is not enough to support a business, so we put in Chinese herbs and Chinese medications. More and more Americans like to use Chinese medicines besides the ginseng root, like tiger balm, cold tablets and cough syrup. Occasionally, American people or Korean people come in and ask for deer horns. A lot of people come in to ask for acupuncture or a Chinese doctor. I say, "I'm sorry. I don't have either one of those."

I'm actually looking forward to retiring as soon as I can. Of course, I don't think I will ever 100 percent retire. I like to work, but not work like what I'm doing now. I'd rather have a few hours for myself. For example, today, I got up about eight o'clock and I will work 'til midnight. If my children were able to take care of some of the businesses I have here, then I would have more time and I don't mind going into some other development, if it suits my interests.

Daniel Hong Lew

Born 1913, Bok Shek Village, Toisan District, Kwangtung Province, China

As soon as I graduated from Broadway High School in 1932, I wanted to go back to China for my university education. This shocked my father. He thought it was absurd because Chinese youth were coming to America to study. Why did I want to go to China to study? When I came here as a boy and saw this wonderful city, wonderful country, I said, "This is what I want for China." Having come from a rural area of China, with all its backwardness, the modern city astonished me with its sanitation, electric lights, running water, automobiles and telephones. There was distinct freedom from fear and superstition. I immediately dreamt of taking back to China these wonderful things that America has in such abundance and helping my native country to modernize like America.

After World War II, I didn't feel that the free world had anything to be able to cope with the Soviet Union. I was glad that NATO was being built in 1949, but NATO was military. I thought this question of Communism needed more than the military. At the United Nations, I felt that the Soviets were drawing circles around us – the free world. I was quite forlorn.

But a most unusual thing happened. I received a telegram passed on to me from Ambassador Wellington Koo, a legendary diplomat. The telegram said that President Chiang Kai-shek had appointed four men to a conference in Michigan. The first three men were quite distinguished – senior Chinese – and the fourth was myself. We were to attend a Moral Rearmament Assembly in Mackinac Island in May, 1955. I said, "My gosh! I'm in such distinguished company! How come?" But what surprised me more was the idea of moral rearmament. I thought what we needed was nuclear rearmament, not moral rearmament, but conferees there were talking about morality and listening to what we Chinese call *Liang Jih*, that voice in you – what they call the guidance of God – and then they talked about wanting to have a different world. To have a different world, we need to have different people, and to have different people, you've got to begin with yourself. I thought, "That's what Confucius talked about – about putting your heart right and then having harmony in the family. When you have that, then you have order in the nation, and with order in the nation, you have world peace." I said, "That's good Chinese philosophy. I'm going to buy this." After that, my diplomatic work became very effective.

We've got to take our hats off to Mao Tse-tung because he lifted the masses up through the organization of the Communist Party. But Communism per se, by itself, is without its values. It's got its economic theory and political theory all right, but where are the values? What are the values that we hold dear – truth, love, kindness, integrity? It's not the material classifications that define the value of man. That's why Chinese culture is inherently so viable and enduring.

Once Mao was able to get the Kuomintang Party and the Nationalist government out, he had the world to himself and his true self emerged. All the worst things began popping up, and no amount of political manipulation could manage that. The values they're trying to bring in now is that you respect authority. Well, that is a kind of value, but what kind of authority? Of course, the Confucian authority is to obey the authority of parents. But nowadays, even the father and mother might make mistakes, too. You cannot be absolute in that respect anymore.

When you come down to it, even though we lost the mainland, even though we've come to Taiwan – a small island – after 40 years, Taiwan has prospered instead of fading away. Why? Because of values. No matter what mistakes Chiang Kai-shek made – and they were political mistakes – he was steadfast in those values.

After completing his early education in Seattle, Daniel Hong Lew studied at several Christian universities in China and at Harvard. Later, adopting the Mandarin name of Yu-Tang D. Lew, he built a distinguished career as a foreign diplomat for the Chinese Nationalist Party in Taiwan. He now teaches young children the wisdom of "Liang Jih" or listening to one's heart.

Sen Poy Chew worked at the Boeing Company for 36 years as a Principle Engineer. Chew is enjoying his retirement by following different health tips and is actively involved with the Guangdong Community Association. He and his wife, Wai Fong, have five children.

Sen Poy Chew

Born August 16, 1933, Fow Sek Village, Toisan District, Kwangtung Province, China

Back in the old days, when Chinese people come to America, they leave their wife and family behind. Once they come to the United States, there's nothing but work. In order to have any social life at all, they come to the association and participate in functions of the association.

I had known about the association when I was a boy. My father belonged so I attended the association's functions many times. Then I had this job at Boeing, so I did not come to the association for many years. Close to retirement, I came back to the association and participated in its various activities.

The Lung Kong Association is a four-family association, and anybody with the last name Lew, Kwan, Jang or Chew automatically belongs. Back in the Han Dynasty, there were four fighters, and they adopted each other as brothers. They had done great deeds for China at that time, so because of their great deeds, people pay remembrance to them. That's the origin of the four-family association. We – the four families – are brothers and sisters, and we will help each other. The creed of the association is *chung, yih, yan, ying,* meaning loyalty, righteousness, kindness and bravery. So aside from trying to practice our creed, we try to do activities that promote friendship among the four family members.

Lung Kong used to be very wealthy. They used to own a building in old Chinatown, on Second and Washington, but back in the 1950s, they sold the place and moved to the new Chinatown. Some of the associations who have their own properties, they will probably continue to exist. But for many associations, like Lung Kong, we don't own property now and we don't have funding other than contributions from the members. It's pretty hard to get the money to pay the rent. Most of the officials in the association are older people. They are either retired now or close to retirement. We are trying to recruit younger members, but we are not too successful.

Since I have become president of the association, my number one goal is to keep the association going. I have added quite a few activities to try to entice people to participate. Back in the early days, there's only one major event. That is the New Year's banquet. Lately, more activities are being added. For instance, we have added in recent years a women's club within the association, and they sponsor the picnic in the summer and a Christmas party. Also, we have a bus tour activity. We select a destination and take a one-day tour.

I feel it is a worthwhile activity. Before I became an official in the association, I did not know that many Chinese people. Now, I do know a lot more.

Gee Min Lee

Born January 8, 1924, Kow Hong Village, Toisan District, Kwangtung Province, China

I came to Seattle in 1951. My father was in Seattle. I also had some relatives – kind of like uncles and cousins – who came to Seattle, too. With all these relatives here, it was easier to make a living. I didn't know a single word of English before I came over here. I had to go to Edison Technical School to learn English. After school, I went to the Wah Young Company where I worked part-time. After three years, I began working full-time. I worked there continuously for 38 years.

If you compare how things were when I arrived with how things are today, it was much more difficult when I arrived. The wages were very low. Attending school part-time cost just over eight dollars a month. There were living quarters and meals at the store where I lived. I would spend a little bit on myself and send money back to Hong Kong to support my family. My wife and my two sons were in Hong Kong. It was very difficult in those days.

In the old days, the family associations had an important role. The Chinese men didn't have a family in the United States. Naturally, they relied on the organizations for various things, including finding a job through the association. Now, it's different. Nowadays, many people have families here. When they get off work, they go straight home.

The group that is taking care of the association now still has some interest in keeping it going. As the group gets older, we, of course, would hand it over to the younger people. The younger people coming from Hong Kong now have very little interest in the association. They have to work and earn a living. If the younger people don't come into the association and help out, the associations will have to close their doors.

Gee Min Lee worked at the Wah Young Company for 38 years before retiring. Ever since his arrival in 1951, he has made sure to visit Chinatown every day. He and his wife have two sons.

Lee Hong "Smiley" Young

Born September 10, 1929, Canton, Kwangtung Province, China
Died 2001, Seattle, Washington

I come from China, 1939. Then I went back to China to get married. It's a blind date. We talked five minute – okay. That's Chinese style. Bring the wife over. My first child was born in '48, the second one in '50, the third one '51. This guy come about '59.

We live at the housing project, up on Yesler Way there. Thirty-five bucks a month. A lot of Chinese people live up there. Like cheap, poor people, they live up there.

My name, I get it from New Chinatown Café. When I working in Hong Kong Café, daytime I work over there and nighttime I go up New Chinatown. Two jobs. I got three sons – tough, so I got to work two job. And one night, one girl say, "Hey, how come you smile so much? What if I change your name to Smiley?" Well, okay, I'll keep that. That's where I get it.

Lee Hong Young worked at many restaurants, including the Hong Kong, New Chinatown, Sun Ya and Trader Vic's Restaurant. He was also a member of the Luck Ngi Musical Club where he played all different types of Chinese and American instruments.

Yu Sung Chin

Born November 22, 1904, Dong On Village, Toisan District, Kwangtung Province, China
Died 2001, Seattle, Washington

My future husband returned to China and used a matchmaker. She would bring a résumé of the prospective brides to give to his mother. If the mother approved, then they would arrange the marriage. After I was married, I had to do everything – cook, wash clothes, make clothes, wash dishes. No one else in my husband's family did anything. I took care of the daily maintenance for the entire family. There was my mother-in-law, father-in-law, a younger uncle, a younger aunt, my husband, myself and my son. There wasn't such an idea of not wanting to do the work. You had to do everything.

I came from Hong Kong in 1951 because mainland China changed their government. A lot of things in America weren't the same as at home. What they wore wasn't the same as what we wore. What they ate wasn't the same. I did not like it. I wanted to go back to China. But because my husband was in the restaurant business, I had to stay and help him. He said that coming to America, everything was not the same as at home. Working in America was very hard. In 1958, I started to go to English school because I did not know how to speak English and was not able to go shopping. It was very hard for me.

I learned to speak, to ride the bus. I learned everything. I could go to the store to buy things. I go downtown to buy materials to make clothing for grandchildren and me. I came to America. I wanted to get my citizenship. This is my adopted homeland.

Yu Sung Chin came to Seattle when she was 49. After struggling with English classes, she finally became a naturalized citizen in 1974.

Gim Chin

Born January 18, 1902, Fuk Lim Village, Toisan District, Kwangtung Province, China
Died February 12, 2000, Seattle, Washington

I never went to school. I don't know how to read. My father said there is no use for girls to study. I never met my husband before we got married. I met him only on the date that we were married. There was not much I could say. I was not in the position to say "yes" or "no." It was my father who made the decision.

I came to the U.S. when I was 57. There were many people coming to the U.S. at that time. I even had a few children when I came to the U.S. We did not get paper for them to come here because it was too expensive. My husband was here for quite some time before I came here. He had been here for over 50 years.

Gim Chin had two boys and two girls, but was not able to join her husband in America until she was 57. Only one of her children, a son, came to the U.S.

Gam Har Chew

Born September 14, 1918, Ai Gong Village, Toisan District, Kwangtung Province, China

My father was 13 years old when he lost his father. There was only one plot of land, which he sold, then he went to Vancouver. He worked in a laundry and did all kinds of odd jobs. He earned some money, then went into business himself and established a successful import-export business.

He was 28 years old when he came back to China to marry my mother. My mother didn't like marrying a man who was this old. After they got married, my father went back to Canada for six years, then returned to China and bought two buildings in Canton City. Japanese planes destroyed the buildings during the War.

As the daughter of a merchant, I was able to go to school, even though I was a girl. I studied Chinese subjects. There weren't any kind of foreign courses. After I studied for several years, my father thought that was enough. He didn't believe girls should get too much education. He wanted girls to stay in the home. To him, what was the purpose of a girl getting an advanced education? She's going to get married anyway, and it's her husband who has to earn money.

I came here in 1950 to join my husband in Seattle, who was working in the laundry business. When I came here, times were very tough. I couldn't find a job. I took a class at the old Edison Technical School for about a month before I had to stop because I had a baby. As I began to give birth to my children – they arrived one year after another – I had no opportunity to continue my classes. Later, after all my children were born and were off to the first grade, I went to work.

In 1960, I went to work at Seattle Glove Company. I learned the job from a Japanese woman who worked there. I earned $1.25 an hour. How pathetic! I made less than $100 a week. Later, I worked at Seattle Quilt Manufacturing Company and Roffe. I worked eight hours at one place during the day, then four hours at another place in the evening. I did finishing work – zippers, sleeves, collars. This was hard work. After work and on the weekends, I took care of the yard and other chores. During this period, my husband was working at the Hong Kong Café. With the two of us working, we were just barely able to make ends meet.

I was over 40 years old when I learned how to drive. We did not have any money to hire someone to teach me, so I practiced in the driveway and in the neighborhood. I was happy when I got my license and I could take my family to the park.

After working nearly 24 years in sewing factories, Gam Har Chew retired in 1984. She and her husband raised one girl and three boys in Seattle.

趙衛金霞

Fung Sinn Wong

Born March 21, 1925, Canton, Kwangtung Province, China

Before I was married, life was pretty good. When the Japanese attacked, we fled to Hong Kong. I was nine or 10. When I was in Hong Kong, I still went to school, but I was very lazy in my studying. Whenever I was in English class, I would read Chinese novels in my lap. I really didn't have any desire to learn English. Sometimes we went to play in the lake, and when we were done, then we went back and school was out. When it came to learning English, I would just get tired. Whenever I see English books, I'll get sleepy. If I had a desire to learn English, then I wouldn't fall asleep.

Even when I was in high school, I never thought that I would go to America. I just thought I would always stay around the village. When I was in school, I had a boyfriend, but my mom didn't allow it because she wanted to go to America.

When I was in China, in school, my mother told me to get married. It wasn't my idea. It was my mother's idea. After I got married, my husband seemed pretty nice. He gave me a lot. When it snowed and my friends asked to play *mah jong*, he shoveled the snow. My husband pretty much gave me the freedom to do what I wanted.

We got married in Hong Kong in 1948 and then came to the U.S. I came to Seattle in 1949. I first started working in 1965. I worked at several places. I sewed. Seventy-five cents per hour. Then after six months, the government raised it to a dollar. Now it would be $6 or $7 an hour. Even if there's nothing to do, now it's $6 an hour. I worked 12 hours a day until my kids graduated.

Fung Sinn Wong worked as a seamstress at many garment factories in Seattle: Black Manufacturing, Farwest Garments Inc., Eddie Bauer Inc., Woolrich and Outdoor Research.

Puey King Wong

Born February 11, 1911, Toisan District, Kwangtung Province, China

I don't know when my husband came over to America. He had been over here for quite a number of years before he went back to China and married me. After the war ended, I came over.

By the time I came over to this country, there were a lot of Chinese arriving here. Men, women and children. A lot of people were coming at the same time. They were mostly related to the U.S. servicemen. My husband had enlisted in the military and had served. He went from America to Japan to the Philippines. As the war was coming to an end, he wanted to go back to China and bring me back here.

I came here in 1947. I started working in 1948. I bought this business from a Mr. Wong. Gradually I learned how to run it on my own. I did everything myself. I didn't have to hire anybody. I didn't have to look for customers. If they wanted to come, then they came. There were whites. There were Filipinos. There were all kinds of people. At that time, most of the customers were Filipino. Business was good back then.

It was very difficult. I had to take in the laundry, repair zippers, do alterations and iron. I had to do some washing and packaging the clean clothes for customers. It was a lot of work. I had to take care of my children at the same time I was working. One would be in a baby carriage and the other would be grabbing on to my sleeve. My husband passed away in 1968. I was the one who single-handedly raised the children.

In 1948, Puey King Wong bought her own laundry, Re-New Cleaners, and ran it by herself for the next 38 years in Seattle's Chinatown. She retired in 1985.

Toy Kay

Born October 17, 1924, Butte, Montana

My mother decided, even when I was 13 years old, that I should marry. At age 15, they found Bill. We met only one time, and in 1941, June 28th, we were married. Bill's younger sister lived in Livingston, Montana, and was married the same way, just a year before our marriage. Her father-in-law, Mr. Wong, a friend of my family, was the matchmaker.

I guess I wasn't really ready for marriage. It was expected of me because this was what my mother just, more or less, preached from the time I was able to hear – that this is the way life is for a girl. Consequently, I couldn't go to high school. I had to get married. It was hard. I came out here and I worked immediately in Kay's Café because they had just started the restaurant in January of that year. My training was to be the obedient daughter-in-law, and I was supposed to please my husband's family. I saved what little tips I did manage to get in the restaurant and bought myself some clothes to go to high school, but I wasn't able to go because my mother said I should forget about that.

Just before Bill sold our restaurant, I decided I wanted to go back to school, so I went to South Puget Sound Community College and passed my G.E.D. Then I went on to college and got my B.A. at Evergreen State College. After that, I was employed by South Puget Sound Community College and became a teacher for English as a Second Language.

Toy Kay is a founding member of the Olympia Area Chinese Fellowship, a friendship organization promoting Chinese culture and heritage. She and her husband, Bill, raised two children.

When the Southeast Asian refugees came, my heart just went out to them. These were people that came and a lot of them were completely separated from their parents. I was volunteering time teaching English at Capitol High School when I saw these young kids that were gaunt, very thin and very confused looking. I thought that I should do something about it.

Gertrude Jue

Born June 12, 1910, Gunnison, Mississippi
Died April 25, 2002, Seattle, Washington

From 1956 to 1960, I worked for the Odion Seafood Company, cracking crab and canning salmon. I would take a bus from Beacon Hill at 6:30 in the morning and get to Pier 66 at 7:45. There were lots of Chinese women working at the cannery. The place was cold and wet every day. Rubber gloves and rubber boots were required and bought by myself for the job. You had to be fast in cracking crabs and get only two breaks a day. It was hard work for the amount of pay. The pay was cheap – 15 cent a pound – and hourly pay was 75 cents an hour. You worked from 8 a.m. to 5:30 p.m., six days a week. You smelled like crab and salmon all the time. It was a hard life, and I only did it to support my four children.

Sponsored by her brother William, Gertrude Jue, pictured on the right, came to America in 1939. She lived in the Milwaukee Hotel and later moved to Beacon Hill with her first husband, Sam Yee. They had four children. Gertrude – better known as Chew Moy Kwai, or Rose, in the Chinese community – divorced Sam and later married Robert Young. She was employed by Odion Seafood Company, Star Laundry and the Bon Marché.

Tsee Watt Mark

Born November 4, 1916, Toisan District, Kwangtung Province, China
Died October 13, 1997, Seattle, Washington

You know, back in those days, there wasn't any paved streets. It was all brick, red brick laid right out there. There was only one person who had a car around here, and that was Mr. Sing Lee. He was a carpenter. He helped build most of the associations. For as many years as I lived here, he was our neighbor. He was like a godfather to me. He took me everywhere with him. He even gave me a tool belt and hammer and took me with him on these jobs. That was a long time ago. Even when I drive by here now, coming down to Chinatown, I always look over here and see that it hasn't changed all that much and remember the good times. It's nostalgia at its best.

Before the Second War, you step in the barbershop, they tell you to get out. They don't cut your hair. If you go into the restaurant, you're not served anything – you're not welcome. Just like the colored people in the South. It's awful bad. No chance to get the job, except working for the family as houseboy and house cook. That's all. No good job for you. Things have changed now. Everything changed. Why did they change it? Because the young generation got more education. More equal rights. The best man wins. You can't get the job done, get out. Before, when I come here, it's terrible.

Kay Ying is for senior citizens. We figure out that all these old people got to find a place to congregate and have a place to read the paper. Before the organization, nobody thinking about getting together. We want to get together, get a place to stay, get a place to help each other, and have fun. The future is good because every year somebody get off the club and somebody get on the club. If you're old enough and you are gone, somebody younger comes up. As long as you're 60 years old, you can get in. Any surname – the Lukes, Mar, Lee or Chew – anybody can get in. Everybody over 60, come in. That's why we got so many members. Now, maybe we have over 700 members. The biggest organization in Chinatown.

Tsee Watt Mark was one of the founders of the Kay Ying Senior Club. The Senior Club provides many of the current Chinese-speaking group a place to meet friends old and new. He is pictured here during World War II.

Ruth Mar

Born September 10, 1913, Los Angeles, California
Died 2000, Seattle, Washington

My husband was going to school at the University of Washington in 1932 when we came up here. He wanted to be an aeronautical engineer. We tried to buy a house and found a nice place on 23rd Avenue near the University. It said, "For rent," so we went and looked, and they wouldn't let us go in. They said, "It's rented already." Then we looked at a house on 27th and Jefferson. In fact, we paid the down payment for the rent and we were ready to move in. Then the door was barred and we couldn't move in. I'm sure it's because of discrimination.

When my husband graduated from the UW [University of Washington], he couldn't get a job. In fact, he went to Boeing School of Aeronautics down in Oakland, California, and Boeing wouldn't hire him. So he just had to do odd jobs until it was the War. That's when many of the Orientals got jobs. I think they were hiring people because of necessity.

Ruth Mar volunteered at Chinese Baptist Church since she and her husband moved to Seattle. In 1936, she and other Chinese women formed the Cathay Matrons Club, a service group that continued until 1991.

As a child, George Ham worked eight to 12 hours a day in his mother's business, the Sun Hing Laundry, on 23rd Avenue and South Jackson Street. After college, he worked as a federal employee inside the Boeing Company for 30 years.

George Ham

Born October 25, 1929, Seattle, Washington

My folks were trying to decide whether to ship the six kids back to China or go open up the laundry. I guess they made the right decision because if we went back to China during the War, I think we'd all be dead. Even though we had to work hard at the laundry, we're still alive.

The laundries were long hours. What you did was you sent the laundry out to be washed and it would come back and you'd do the rest. Like starching the shirts, drying them, ironing the collars and cuffs. And then you'd iron the rest of the body of the shirts. At times, my parents worked 16 hours a day.

It just happened that we had a house just around the corner from the laundry, so at least they knew where we were. Most of the time, we were at the laundry anyway — ironing from anywhere from eight to 12 hours or more a day to get the shirts done.

I think the old people were smart enough. They recognized that they don't want their kids to go to the laundries, so they sent them to school and got them educated. I went to Seattle University and majored in accounting. When I got out of school in 1953, for eight months I could not get a job. Discrimination still existed. So with a degree, I ended up working for Northwestern Mutual Insurance Company in the stock room. With a degree. That's the only job I could get.

With discrimination, if you were a minority, the old saying is: "You don't have a Chinaman's chance." They look at you, take your application, and probably pitch it as soon as you walk out the door. They just don't hire. The only reason that the minorities got a break was during World War II. For example, Boeing had a contract with the government, and right in the contract, there was a no-discrimination clause. It finally broke their back and they had to hire. If it wasn't for that, I don't think there'd be anybody out there yet.

I have two girls and two boys. I promised all four kids at least four years of college, but I didn't soft-sell them on going to school. If you don't have that education, you don't have something to offer. You will not make it because of the discrimination, which is still out there. When the times get tough, you've got more people that are out there stabbing you in the back. Everybody is looking for that almighty dollar. If you are equal with a Caucasian, your chances of making it are not good. They're going to pick the white over you. You've got to be twice as good as them if you want to move ahead.

I'm still putting three square meals on the table every day and I got a roof over my head. You don't go out and buy a new car and go out and do a lot of things, but you go ahead and spend the money on the kids' education. You may not be able to give them money, but at least you give them an education. I feel that's important — that they really have some skills and tools to go out and compete. It's a dirty world out there. You have to go out and compete. You've got to learn to survive.

Frances Chin Ho

Born May 13, 1917, Seattle, Washington

I attended elementary school in Vancouver, Washington. And at this time, Vancouver was just beginning to have a few farm homes on the highway. I lived with my mother's sister and her husband and my cousins. There was an awful lot of hard work for the youngsters, and yet, I don't regret that. At that time when we go and harvest strawberries, we would pick the biggest and ripest ones. To us, that was happiness – and we would rave about it. Responsibilities galore were ours, that's true, but we did have a lot of happy moments.

After World War II, I could see that people weren't racially conscious at all. In my time, even going to a theater, I had this experience in Seattle. There were hardly any customers there, but

When she was young, Frances Chin Ho's grandmother told her, "Why do girls need an education? In the end, you have to do diapers." Ho felt those were "fighting words." She put herself through the University of Washington by working in a grocery store she purchased from a Japanese American couple interned during World War II. After college, she moved to Hawaii and taught at public schools in Pahoa and Hilo. She retired in 1975. She still lives in Hawaii and attributes her long life to walking three miles a day.

they sent us up to the balcony just because we were Chinese. I thought the place was filled, but I looked down and there was no one there. I felt that this was racial discrimination.

You get the feeling you weren't always welcome at certain restaurants. I remember that I wrote letters to different restaurants and I said, "If you are racially discriminating, please let me know. I won't go and I'll tell my friends not to come." And that happened several times. It's very interesting, but one store would phone another store to see if I had complained before. I didn't feel that we were really that equal. It's after World War II that everybody became more democratic.

For some reason or other, there was all this talk about girls don't get an education, and because they said this so much, I found myself challenged. Girls entering college at that time was not the most popular thing to do, especially if you were Oriental. Some *haole* girls were going, but the enrollment was still small. In fact, many colleges did not accept girls. It's only in the last two, three decades that we have co-education for both boys and girls.

I had the opportunity to invest because of the evacuation. The people were going to camp, Japanese people in Seattle. The Butte Grocery was located on Yesler Hill. The owners, knowing that I wanted to go to the UW [University of Washington], said, "This is a great opportunity, whereby you won't have to worry about tuition or anything. The store will provide enough and more than enough." So I really got not only my education, but I was able to travel.

I got a B.A. in literature in 1945, and in '47, an M.A. in Spanish, American and English literature. When I got my master's, I said I was going to treat myself to an odyssey of some kind, and I came to Hawaii because the weather was warm. I kind of felt, too, at that time, there was still racial discrimination. It's only after World War II that there's a flood of everybody going into different jobs in Seattle or the West Coast. At that time, I still think it was rare to be hired for a teaching job here.

We have one daughter, but I feel she was deprived of a lot of things I went through that were enriching. I had gone to the farm and I worked hard. I know what hardship is and I know what it means to use your muscles and I know what a tired body means. It was tough, but it builds character. I worked my way through school, but she doesn't have to worry about tuition. All she has to do is, "Mom and Dad, I need this," and we send the money. We did try to give her the responsibility of working a little bit. That gave her some idea of working, but that kind of work is sophisticated compared to what I had to do. So she was deprived of some things I think are important in molding character. But not only her, all the people of her generation.

Vincent Y. Dong

Born January 5, 1927, Seattle, Washington

There was a large Japanese population that lived on 17th and 18th and Yesler, areas around there, so when I first started in high school, maybe half of the kids were Japanese. If you look in our yearbook, say, the class of '41, you see a lot of Japanese faces, but if you look in the graduating class of '45, not a single Japanese face. And, of course, you know why, if you're familiar with the history of World War II, because they were all sent to internment camps. And that includes some of my friends from that period.

In junior high school, or maybe even elementary school, three of us — myself, Chinese, a Japanese fellow and a Jewish fellow — formed a club together. We called it the Three Comrades. We even had a motto and designed little badges. It lasted up through high school, but that shows how long our friendship lasted. My Japanese friend, of course, was among those whose family was uprooted and had to leave for the camps.

The war in China started in July, 1937, and one of the things the Chinese did in Seattle was to urge a boycott of Japanese goods that were flowing to the United States. This was before Pearl Harbor, so the United States and Japan were still engaged in commerce with each other. So we would organize demonstrations and do some picketing. We would parade on the piers. We knew about the Japanese atrocities committed against the Chinese in the war, but I don't recall that I ever took back this feeling directly to my friends who were Japanese.

During the war years, I joined the debate team and participated in oratorical contests. We would have war bond drives, and I would go up there and speak to urge students to buy war bonds. Now that I look back, perhaps it is kind of interesting from the viewpoint of other students that an Asian was able to do this. Throughout my life, I guess I've done a lot of things and I'm the only Asian. I didn't really find that unusual. Many times my dad would ask me if I've done something or gone to a meeting and he would say, "Are you the only Chinese there?" And I would say, "Yes, I'm the only Chinese there." And he wouldn't say anything,

After earning his master's degree in journalism, Vincent Dong went to work as a social sciences editor for the World Book Encyclopedia in Chicago in 1956. After his marriage in 1961, he moved to California and began a new job as editor in the research branch of the U.S. Forest Service. He is pictured at center with his brothers and sisters, circa 1949.

but I could tell by the way he reacted and the look in his eyes that he felt proud that I was as good as the *bok guey*, white devils.

After my wife and I were married, we decided that we would settle in San Francisco, and of course, one of the first things we started looking for was an apartment. We went to the want ads and saw this particular apartment, and I knew that this apartment was just right around the corner – maybe half a block. So we went to a phone booth and I called this person and said we'd like to come around. And we were told, yes, it was still for rent. So we started walking toward the apartment and we started to ascend the set of stairs and this fellow opened the doors. I said, "Sir, I understand you have an apartment for rent." And he took one look at us and said, "No, sir. It was just rented." Now remember this was just within minutes after I phoned the guy. What could you say? My wife looked awfully bewildered – she couldn't understand what was going on. She had not been in this country that long and had not experienced the things I had experienced. I was kind of used to this by now. I explained to her that very likely we were turned down because we were Chinese. She told me that she felt like someone had slapped her in the face.

It's basically a white society. Notwithstanding this attempt for diversity and so forth, it will always remain a white society as long as we live in this country. Even though whites will constitute less than 50 percent of the work force in the year 2000, the real power – the economic, financial and political power – will not basically change in my lifetime. This is why I encourage our children to get the best education they can to make a better life for themselves.

Art Louie

Born July 22, 1918, Seattle, Washington

I don't know how we all got so interested in fishing, but I remember my younger brother, Kenny, and I, when we were eight, nine and 10, we used to walk two to three miles down to Lake Union to go fishing. I think in those days, it was very typical that the father didn't do things with their kids. It was a normal way of life. I think my father was influenced by the old traditional Chinese ways. I don't think there were many fathers at that time that ever took their kids out fishing, took them to football games and stuff like that.

My dad wanted me to go to Chinese school and I finally went, but I was 15 and about as tall as I am now, and we were in the first grade, in Chinese school. So all the other kids except for this other fellow who was the same age as I was – Wilson Mar – everybody else was six years old. Boy, was that a tough deal. So I didn't learn very much Chinese.

We always had this one picture of my dad – I don't know whether I should be saying this, but it was really quite an interesting story.

My nephew, Greg, was back in New York and this friend called him up and said that he had a picture that he wanted to show him. It was an old *Seattle Star* newspaper, 1934. He found it as a backing in a mirror that he was unpacking. The picture on the front page was of my dad being taken off to the federal pen. I got a kick out of it because he looked like Eliot Ness. I always remembered that when we went to visit him, it was all wide open. He was there for six months. I always wanted to show that picture to my better friends. I thought it was great. I don't look down on the fact that my dad was a gambler. I think he was a hell of a guy for doing what he did with as little education as he had. In those days, it was tough for Chinese to make a move. He did what he had to for his family's sake.

There were two instances of discrimination which played a part in my life. One was when I was 17. I went with three *lo fan* [white] kids to play golf at Maplewood. They wouldn't let us on because I was Chinese. I don't think it bothered me as much because I always knew there was discrimination and I always felt that it wasn't going to do me any good to fight it. I just kind of accepted it. And then the other instance was when I went to buy a house. It was 1951 and I had some idea to live on the lake. I was buying this house and I talked to the real estate guy and he was fine. He wanted to sell it to me, but the neighborhood came out with a petition. They didn't want us to buy, but we had already bought it. All the people down there finally became our friends, the same ones that signed the petition. I didn't let those things bother me at all. I felt that this is the way they are and maybe I can help change their thinking a little bit. And I think I have, not only I, but I think my family at that time also helped change things.

I studied a year and a half in sculpturing with Dudley Pratt, who was considered one of the real good art teachers, but then I went into the sporting goods business and I didn't do anything with art. Then finally, I became influenced a little bit by Paul Horiuchi, whose paintings I was interested in. I bought a couple and helped him sell some. It made me think when I saw his work that I could do that. So I spent about the first year when I started playing around with art doing collage. I always felt that for me, it wasn't very difficult. I just wasn't challenged until William Ivy, who is considered the foremost abstract painter in the Northwest, was going to teach down at Highline College. I went down there and joined the class. Because he was such a good teacher, I've been fairly successful in abstract painting. He helped me figure out if I could paint, what the reasons were behind it and if I could paint professionally. I've probably sold 175 paintings all over. I have been painting now for 24 years and I never tire of it. It's very challenging.

Art Louie owned and operated Hab's Sporting Goods in Chinatown from 1943 to 1961. He operated Art Louie's Restaurant at Seventh Avenue and King Street from 1962 to 1970, and Art Louie's Uptown at Fourth Avenue and Virginia Street from 1969 to 1977. He plays golf, fly fishes and paints in his spare time, displaying his work in a gallery in West Seattle.

Keye Luke

Born 1904, Canton, Kwangtung Province, China
Died January 12, 1991, Los Angeles, California

I just had a natural talent that developed. When my father passed away, I converted into commercial art and made a good living. Among the younger generation, I was the first Chinese to go into the mainstream as an artist in Seattle. From there, I did motion picture advertising for the Columbia Theater. It was in Seattle, Second and Pike. It was the chief theater in the Carl Laemmle chain of Northwest Theaters.

I went down to Hollywood because a friend of mine was a writer for Charlie Chaplin. He came to Seattle for vacation and says, "Oh, come to Hollywood. That's where the action is." I wound up with an advertising art agency doing commercial artwork. Then, that same year, I went back to Seattle and did a series of Chinese murals for the Bon Marché. They had a new building then. And those murals were up there for years. Then I left in 1927 and haven't been back.

I don't know why other Asians should want to follow in my footsteps, as an actor, but if they do, it's all right. But let me tell you that when I started out, there was only a handful, and I had

powerful friends within the business that opened doors for me. Some of these people were publicity experts like Hedda Hopper, Louella Parsons, Jimmie Star, Harrison Carroll. When they heard that I was going to be an actor, because they already knew me because of my artwork, they gave me publicity that money could not buy. They boosted me at every turn. That was an advantage I don't think any Asian ever had.

You see, it's a matter of time and place. I'm not saying that I was good. I was all right. I did the work, and they accepted me and bought me, but I was lucky. Friends helped me. No Chinese kid today has friends powerful enough in the business to help them. But if they still want to be an actor, then be prepared for a long life of unremitting devotion to something that may bring them joy at times when they get a good part, but mainly disappointment and waiting, waiting, waiting for that chance. Because there are so few of them, and the demand is so few. Like everything else, you're a minority in a country that's a majority white. And it's a white man's theater and they're interested in white subjects and you're in a secondary category.

The Chinese actor has limited opportunities. But if he is prepared to devote his whole time, his whole life to this art form, then I would say, "Stay in it." But don't expect it to give you the things that you think you should get because life is a matter of luck. It flits around like a spring butterfly. You may be lucky and get a good part now, and you may be unlucky and lose a good part to some competitor. So there's nothing sure about it. The only thing that's sure is that if you are lucky enough to get good parts and get a good reputation, you will climb in it and become valuable in it. They will buy you because you're good, but don't count on it.

I haven't had any disappointments because I have never set my sights on anything that I couldn't obtain. I've tried to be very rational and realistic and accept the things that have come my way. I just finished a picture, which I think is the most important picture I've ever done, as far as the motion picture business is concerned – Woody Allen's new picture, "Alice," which they just released.

My role is that of a Chinese American herbalist. He's in New York's Chinatown, and he's a combination of Oriental medicine and Western medicine, and personal character and personal lifestyle is a blend of both. In other words, he's a true character out of American soil. A combination of Eastern and Western elements, and it's as true to life as can be.

In 1927, Keye Luke left Seattle to go to Hollywood. He eventually appeared in over 100 films during an acting career spanning 56 years. He was best known as Detective Charlie Chan's "Number One Son" in nearly a dozen films and Master Po in the television series, "Kung Fu." In 1990, he became the fourth Asian American to receive a star on the Hollywood Boulevard Walk of Fame. He is pictured at center in the 1937 film, "The Good Earth."

Helen Eng Kay's grandfather was an herbalist who worked with Dr. Ing Hay, the legendary frontier "China Doctor" in John Day, Oregon. Kay grew up in Newport, Washington, but moved to Seattle to attend the University of Washington. Married to Richard Kay, both are retired owners of the Hall-O'Leary Pharmacy since 1997. She serves on the King County Board of Equalization/Appeals and has been a long-time supporter and board member of the Wing Luke Asian Museum.

Helen Eng Kay

Born September 24, 1935, Lewiston, Idaho

My mother and father worked so much in the restaurant, the Newport Café, which was American and Chinese. There was an American menu, then we had things like chow mein with the crispy noodles. My father would make the noodles himself – he would fry them rather than have them sent. It was a lot of work – he was a good cook. My father died when I was 16 and my brother was eight, so mother had to raise two children, and the only thing she knew was to carry on with the restaurant. And that's what she did so that my brother and I could go to college. She was only 32 when she was widowed.

We were required to work in the restaurant. I remember getting up at five in the morning and waiting tables eight to 10 hours a day after I was 12 years old. I never felt I had a childhood. Education was also very important. Even though we were isolated in Newport, it was expected that I go to college. Out of a class of 45 – ours was the largest class because the Newport area was so countrified – there were only six of us going to college.

Since we were the only Chinese family in town, we did not really learn much about Chinese customs. My father would say that it was Chinese New Year, and you know, that's fine – it's Chinese New Year – but it wasn't anything significant to me personally. My mother-in-law was very much the opposite. She grew up in a family that was steeped in customs. She was Americanized because she was born here, but at the same time, my mother-in-law knew everything about Chinese customs. My first inkling was when Dick and I were to be married, and she said we had to have these Chinese customs. Those things were observed because mother Lew Kay wanted to do them. She said you had to pour tea and you get a present, and I said, "Wow! Pouring tea is going to get me a present!" I was glad to do it! We were getting married in Newport, and my mother-in-law brought all these teacakes. She was going to bring a roasted pig, but the relative who was going to bring it over was unable to attend. I think there was even $99. Marriage observation with the nines signify eternity. My grandfather was kind of superstitious. He picked the marriage date. It had to be a good day. I thought it was kind of silly, but I went along with it. What the heck, it's not going to hurt anything.

After we were married, we did it Chinese style. I lived in his house for two years before we got our home. Dick has only lived in two homes all his life. So I lived with my mother-in-law for two years, and after she sold her house, she came and lived with us.

She was Americanized and a Christian, so she knew it was superstition, and yet she kind of liked to carry the New Year's customs out. I think it was because she was raised that way. So we couldn't sweep the floor, and she would cook dinner, and we would save half the chicken for the next day. Start with the whole chicken. And when the baby was born, we'd have the *gai jow* [whiskey chicken], black vinegar pig feet and the pink eggs. Those are things we still observe.

I feel there was some discrimination when we tried to find a home. I think they selectively took us to places on Mercer Island that they thought it would be "safe" to put Asians because we were one of the first. There weren't too many, other than Dick's aunt, who had been there a long time ago.

Ruby Chow

Born June 6, 1920, Seattle, Washington

We were just going by this place and there was that location right on Broadway and Jefferson. It was an Italian restaurant, a house converted to a restaurant. I don't know what made me say it, but I said, "This is the place I would like to start a restaurant." It's in a residential area. Ping said, "Well, fine. As long as we make enough to take care of the kids, that's all that matters."

We went there with $100 in our pockets, and we put two $20 ads in the newspapers – one in the *Post-Intelligencer* and one in the *Seattle Times*. Our plan was that I would work the dining room and Ping would be in the kitchen with a helper to help him with the cooking and washing the dishes. We were intending to run the place with three people. The day we opened, we never stopped. It was packed every day.

Weekends would be the local people. Monday to Friday would be mostly people from out of town. What I learned is that people, when they go out to dine, they want to be served. And when you give them good service, and when you're sincere about it, and when you work hard and make sure that they're taken care of, people will pay for it.

In 1949, the Seafair Festival started and the local Chinese invited the girls from Victoria to march in the Seafair Parade. They had a drill team up there. When I looked at that, I felt we had enough Chinese girls to do that and we should try and start a program. At first, when the girls came to me, there was only a group of 25 girls. I said, "There are only 25 of you, but in order to go out as a drill team, you must have more than 25 to make it look good." That was on the advice of the police officer that was helping us, but they didn't want to let any other girls into the organization. I said, "Well, if I do anything, it will have to be for any girl that wants to be of service to the community."

We went back to Hong Kong and we got the costumes. I carried 40 of them – 40 headdresses back, and they were confiscated from me when I came through customs. After they took everything away from me, I called Howard McGowen who was down there as collector of customs the next day. He says, "Ruby, what are you trying to smuggle through?" I said, "I'm not trying to smuggle through. I'm bringing this for the community. See what you can do to help." He got them back for us and that's how we got the first set of costumes in. That's where we started the drill team.

I would like to see a community center go up for the youth. I've been working on it since 1975, when we bought that piece of property in the back of the Chong Wa Benevolent Association. It's a very desirable area for a gym, a big place where young people can get together and we could have functions for the elders. I would like to see it get off the ground because it's badly needed. People have the concept that the Chinese people don't need any help, but we do. We have problems coming up. Once you get into a large city, you have more problems.

For 30 years, Ruby Chow and her husband, Ping, operated Ruby Chow's Restaurant on Seattle's Capitol Hill. She formed the Chinese Community Girls' Drill Team in 1951 and has been an active leader in the Chong Wa Benevolent Association for many years. In 1973, she won election to the King County Council and served for 12 years.

周馬雙金

Art Lum attended Seattle University on the G.I. Bill. He married Helen Lee, a Seattle native, after the two met in Portland. From 1958 to 1988, Lum worked as a structural engineer at the Boeing Company. He has spent many years as director and manager of the award-winning Chinese Community Girls' Drill Team.

林炳達

Art B. Lum

Born August 3, 1923, Canton, Kwangtung Province, China

I don't know when my father came to this country. I think he worked in the farms and maybe on the railroads. I think he's first in Colorado and maybe he's in Utah. And then he went to California – I don't know what year. He never tells me these things. I think he settled in Marysville, California, and that's where I spent my teenage years in school when I came to this country. My mother never did come over to this country. I don't know why, but maybe she didn't want to. She died pretty early, right after the war.

My first memory of America is pretty strange. I was 16 or 17, somewhere around there. Just when I entered San Francisco, you're an immigrant and you get locked up for a few days and that's kind of strange. But everything turns out. They didn't really mistreat people very badly. Just ask questions and then they release you. I didn't have any problems at all. I was there maybe only a couple of weeks or so. I was very fortunate. My dad was supposed to be born here. Because the immigration law in San Francisco – earthquake, fire – so all those people become citizens. So actually, I am a citizen, too.

I joined the Chinese Community Service Organization in 1970 and was elected the president in 1975 and 1980. CCSO is to help Chong Wa Benevolent Association do some of their activities. We did a lot of things for the community. For instance, during the year I was there, we published a health manual to help the Chinese to pass the health test to get a health license without speaking English. Before that, they put in some street lanterns in Chinatown, and that street bulletin board on the corner of Seventh and King – that's a CCSO project.

One of the most memorable things to me is the CCSO Summer Youth Program. Every year during the summer, we sponsor a program for youth, ages 13 to 16. We have summer activities for them, and we have classroom activities, teach them Chinese, bilingual teaching. And then we take them to the park and take them roller-skating and all those things.

All my life, I've always been working with youth. Everybody knows me as "Uncle Art." I was Cub Scout master. Then, I was at the Summer Youth Program and the Chinese Girls' Drill Team. My real satisfaction is to see the development of all those youth. They turn out – most of them – to be very good citizens. We have drill team members turn out like Cheryl Chow. She's a City Council person. We have some engineers and we have some advertising executives and we have some bankers and we have some accountants. A lot of professional people. That's really rewarding – to at least see them go through high school.

I think my goal is to continue on, to serve the community as drill team director until I feel like I should retire. I received the "Unsung Hero" award from the Japanese American Citizens League in 1982. That's exactly what it meant – unsung hero – because I don't get any other award like that, not even from our community.

Larry Chinn worked as a quality control supervisor at the Boeing Company for over 30 years. After he retired in 1977, he returned to his boyhood interest of kitemaking. He won many awards for his colorful Chinese hand-painted animal kites. He was an original member of the Chinese Art Club, a Chinatown organization started in 1936.

陳培元

Lawrence P. Chinn

Born October 9, 1914, Canton, Kwangtung Province, China
Died May 4, 1994, Seattle, Washington

I remember part of my childhood in the old country. When I was a kid in China, from April to September during the nice weather time, we have lots of fun flying kites, and that's how I learned, from the older people. All the youngsters build the kites and paint them and so on. We had a lot of fun flying them. Just before going back to school, we tied the punk to the line and burned it off and let the kites fly away in the pasture, and nobody would pick them up. Kind of superstitious. Supposedly, the bad luck would fly away with the kite.

I came over in 1931, May fourth. I came over on the President Jefferson. I took about a month to get over here, including a stop by Japan. My first impression was the 42-story building – the Smith Tower. That was the tallest building at that time and it really stood out. Before we docked, I saw all the buildings were so much more modern and better looking than in Canton City. I stayed in immigration until May ninth, then I was released and came out. All the time, my dad and my brother, Lincoln, was able to go down to immigration and say hello to me.

My sister back in New York sent for me and told me that I can get a part-time job and go to school and learn a trade. For 18 months, I was back in New York. I went to Roosevelt Aviation School, going through all of the phases of construction and testing and so on. I also like to learn how to fly an airplane. I did spend some time on learning. I couldn't afford to keep on going because it cost quite a bit of money to learn. At that particular time, it costs around $12 an hour for small, single engine airplane, so I decided to learn how to be an A&E mechanic – airplane and airplane engines. I started at Boeing in 1943.

When my son, Clayton, was in Cub Scouts, we had a contest of kite flying and building competition, and I built five kites for him to go into competition. I built a butterfly, and an eagle, and a centipede, and a blue bird, and so on. He won some prizes from the Cub Scout competition, but he was never too interested in it. So in later years, I give them away. But after I retire, and kite flying now getting so popular and getting so broad all over the world, I decided to go back, building a lot of kites. I've been invited to schools to show the children, exhibit my kites, and show them how to build the simple things.

I have built about 300 or more kites. Each individually hand-painted and constructed. I use at least three different materials. For structure, I use wooden dowels and bamboo. For covers, I use nylon and paper. Three layers. Real strong stuff, that's good for painting. That's how my Chinese kites are made, so I can paint them with acrylic paint. I build the kites like the owls and goldfish with the eyes spinning.

Eddie Moy was a long time waiter at Tai Tung Restaurant in Seattle's Chinatown. People would come far and wide and would always ask for Eddie, saying, "I want Eddie!" He retired in 2002 after over 50 years at the restaurant.

Eddie Moy

I worked continuously in the restaurants. I've been at Tai Tung for over 40 years. When I first started working here, there wasn't much business. It was mostly Filipinos, Blacks and a few Chinese. The wages were not very high. The tips were very low, too. You would be overjoyed if you got 50 cents tip. At that time, for example, a party of Filipinos returning from Alaska with 20 or 30 some people filling up two dining rooms, you got two dollars in tip. Sometimes two dollars, sometimes three dollars. Wow! That was a lot! If you earned five dollars for two days, it was considered fortunate. At that time, the meals were much cheaper, too. It's very different now.

The menu is different. At that time, a noodle dish was about a dollar. Nowadays, an order of egg foo young is five dollars. Back then, it was $1.25. Chow mein was also about $1.75. Tomato beef was a dollar or something. Pretty cheap. I don't remember all the old dishes. They don't prepare them anymore.

Working here, occasionally when the customers give birth to children, have weddings or graduations, I invite them to dinner and send some flowers. When they have a birthday, I give a special meal to them. On special days like Christmas time, I come back here to make almond cookies to send out to everybody. I make the almond cookies, I pay for the almond cookies, and I bring them up to everybody. I give it to the customers. That's how they know me. I'm a good friend of everybody. Here, everyone asked for me when they first came in: "Eddie! Eddie!" Those who didn't know me would ask, "Who's Eddie?" Those who knew me said, "Eddie, I want you to take care of me."

Seattle has changed. Even if you had a whole day, you couldn't describe it all. In the old days, people were out 24 hours a day. The Chinese weren't afraid of anything. You could walk until dark. No danger, no nothing. No one disturbed anybody. The hotels also had good business. Everybody came to Chinatown to live. Nowadays, by eight o'clock, it's pretty quiet. No people walk around.

In the old days, there weren't as many police as there are now. In the old days, the police hardly had to do anything. It was peaceful. There were Blacks, Chinese, whites. They filled the streets! The cars could hardly pass. All the Chinese restaurants were always open. They all opened until five or six in the morning. It was great! The old days were better than right now. Nowadays, people stay home. They don't dare to step outside at night. In the old days, everybody drove down here. People from other states came here on vacation. They all came down to visit Chinatown. Everything has changed. Before, Chinatown was prosperous.

Now, the thinking is different. Back then, you helped me and I helped you. If you had any kind of problem, everybody knew about it. Whatever you did, everybody would know. Everyone would do things for free because everyone was a good friend. Everyone had relatives. Nowadays, you don't dare ask anyone for help. Nowadays, if you ask for something, people will ignore you. In the old days, you came over from China and everybody helped everybody. Nowadays, the attitude is "I don't know you and you don't know me." Nobody knows anybody else.

Henry Louie

Born February 24, 1925, New York, New York

It's a funny thing. You look through the United States – most of the Chinatowns are close to train stations. Now, that gives you a clue that when the Chinese first came over, they worked on the railroads, and also they catered to the people – hand laundries and so forth. You look down in San Francisco, the first Chinatown was close to the train station. Same thing up here. Same thing in Portland.

I think business is moving upwards, going toward 12th Avenue because they could expand it out without any restrictions, almost. But here in Chinatown, too conservative – cannot get any people to come here and invest. You cannot tear the old buildings down.

Since we are doing our business in Chinatown, we like to see Chinatown grow. Naturally, as a businessman, I'd like to see more business and I guess we have to coexist with some of those low-cost housing people. A lot of people like to see more low-cost housing while businessmen like to see more new business. Any kind of business that would increase people coming down here, draw people's interests – souvenirs, curio shops, things like that.

We could have probably gotten a lot bigger building for Tsue Chong, more efficient building over in Kent, but the city treated us so nicely that we're just going to stay here during the interim period. We have been placed under the Seattle School System as an audio-visual program, and we kind of feel fortunate about that because we have a chance to expose Chinatown to the school kids – show them how the other people from other part of the world lives and how they make their living. So, I think we like to stay in Chinatown as long as possible. But when it comes to the point where we have to move, then probably we have to move out.

Henry Louie earned an engineering degree at the University of Washington in 1950. He worked as a Boeing engineer for several years before joining his brother, Ken, full-time at their grandfather's business, the Tsue Chong Company, a noodle and fortune cookie factory in Chinatown.

Dan Mar

Born August 16, 1925, Seattle, Washington

Dan Mar served in the U.S. Navy from 1943 to 1946 as an electrician, Third Class. He was also part of the first All-Chinese American group in the Navy and has been a longtime leader in the Cathay Post #186 of the American Legion. In 1971, he started Pacific Components Inc. which is located in the same building as Marpac Construction, run by his two sons. Married to Edith, they have two sons and two daughters.

Chinatown, as we knew it, is going to pass. Chinatown, as it will be in the future, will still be a Chinatown. There'll be all the rest of the Southeast Asians who have come in, and all of the people who are coming in. At one time, everybody in Chinatown knew everybody. We all spoke the same dialect, the same language. But now you go down into Chinatown, Toisanese is becoming extinct.

We used to live three miles away from Chinatown. That's where the social center was. That's where people that you knew, that you worked with, you went to school with, they all lived down there. There was a reason for going down there. Now, what is the reason for going down there? Nobody that I know lives in the area. There's no schools down there. The doctors we go to see are someplace else, the dentist we see is someplace else, the barber we go to is someplace else.

I don't think we should think that we should keep the status quo. It's going to change. Right now, very few empty stores down there, but there are no mainstream type of business – all little shops, boutique shops, video stores, restaurants, but nothing really substantial to draw people down there and make it a complete community. I realize that low-cost housing is a necessity, but does the whole community need to be low-cost? I don't think so. We got to improve the whole area at one time. You just can't keep it as low-income. We do need to help the businesses who are there to prosper. We do need to keep the image of Chinatown alive. We need to make sure.

We talk about improving Chinatown or making it a more livable place. Without people living there you can't do it. Unless you get people living there, kids walking the street, people walking the streets, you just don't have a community.

Steven Luke

Born September 26, 1931, Yen An Lee Village, Toisan District, Kwangtung Province, China

In the old days, most of the Chinese people are single. They don't have families in here. The associations are the easier way for the single people to get together. In the old days, the associations have boarding rooms. People actually stay in the association. Some stay so many years looking for job. When the Lukes come to the United States, the first seaport they live in is Seattle. When they first come from China, they need the place to stay, so the association is the place that provides them the room and board until they find a job or go some other place.

Most of the Chinese when they first come, work in the laundry. When I first come in 1949, my first job is in the laundry. In the old days, the Lukes are mostly working in the laundries, and then later, they moved into the restaurant business. Laundries are mostly hard labor work. Naturally, when you first come in, lack of knowing the language, you don't have any connections, where else can you go? Your relatives, your father, your grandfather work in the laundry, the only place you can go is work in the laundry.

The future of this association is very gloomy because financially our association entirely depends on our members' contributions. All the associations are pretty poor except those that have income, the ones that have a building and then build up their money. The others – it's all through the private donations from their members. The only income is through this: the private donations, plus all the weddings. Every year, as a member of the association, you ask to donate so much money. Sometimes people feel very happy for the wedding, so they say, "Okay, let's donate some money to the association." Through sad things like funerals, they do donate some money to remember the deceased one. These are the only income, so the income is pretty limited because only the older folks nowadays are doing that. The younger generation – like your generation – you hardly even go in to see the association at all. There's no income from the younger generation. But the older people pass away one by one, so you can see the income is limited.

For all the associations, pretty much about the same, it's still the people that come from China that run it. The younger people, very, very few of them participate. They only go to the banquets. On the day-to-day gatherings, only the older folks. Of course, the younger people have to work, too. You can't expect the younger people to be able to go to the associations and play *mah jong* and do a little bit of talking like that. You people have to go to work. It's quite understandable.

For me, I feel that the family association has a good purpose – to help the younger people to remember the older generation, the way they come and the way they struggle, the way they bring up the kids. I think it's very important. To me, working in the association is trying to bring more activities to the younger people, to make it more interesting to the younger people. Hopefully, in the future, the younger people will understand the past and develop into a better American citizen and show that the Chinese people are really hardworking people.

Steven Luke is the former president of the Hoh Nam Association. This family association consists of those with the last names of Luke, Shue and Liu and originates from Northern China. Luke hopes that the family association will help the younger generations remember the older generations - the way they came, their struggle and their lives.

Homer Wong's father was made the mayor of Chinatown by then Seattle Mayor John F. Door in 1932. At the age of 65, Wong retired from the Washington State Liquor Board. He is currently an active member at the Bing Kung Association.

黃篤榮

Homer Wong

Born 1919, Seattle, Washington

I have been going to the Wong Association since I was a child. When I was born, my father already put my name in there as another member of the Wong family when he pays dues for us every year. Whenever a certain occasion come up, we always go down there to participate.

The family association was to keep the Wong people together, more or less a family get-together. All the Wongs, all the Woos, and all the Chins, they all have their own family association. It is more or less sticking together with their family down there. If you're a Wong and if you need help and some Wongs are working, they might hire another Wong to work for them. If you were the owner of a business, you would try to hire some of your relatives to work for you.

I go to the Wong Association because I feel that it is my duty to go down there and participate in order to keep the family association alive. If everyone don't get involved in it, then it would be dissolved and we don't know what would happen after that.

The tong is more or less a protector of the Chinese people. In the early days, they had different tongs. They have their own gambling places, and they protect their own people. In the early days, the Chinese in America was more or less mistreated, and this tong was organized to protect the Chinese people from other people who want to beat them up.

This is not the same kind of tong like in the past. They're mostly older people. They come here to read the newspaper, they come here and watch television, and they can come here and chew the fat. We have parties – not very often, but certain occasions we do. New Year's is the biggest. They generally have dinner down here. For midnight, they have everybody be here to start celebrating New Year's. Every year, we have to pay dues, otherwise we won't be able to maintain the operation. None of the younger generation likes to come to those tongs down there now.

It eventually will fade away. Nobody wants to come down here. You have your own friends to get together with, I have my own friends to get together with. You don't have to come down to the Wong's anymore to get together. It's a new era. The future generation, you don't find very many of them will be speaking Chinese or anything like that. I'm one of the few American-born that still speak Chinese because I was brought up with Chinese, but my grandchildren aren't going to do that. They are speaking English all the time, they don't speak Chinese. Give them a couple more generations, they'll all wander off into a different world.

James Yee

Born October 24, 1927, Sueylung Village, Toisan District, Kwangtung Province, China

I was brought up by my father and the people around him. I mingled with people that are associated with the family association. In the early days, it is supposed to be able to help the various Yees that cannot speak English. You can call it a fraternity or self-help type organization. They treat each other like brothers and sisters.

I come from the old country in the first place, so I have that touch of Chinese culture. I treasure the roots. I appreciate what the older generation gone through and these associations that helped them in the past. There's a lot of heritage involved in this kind of organization. It's good for the young people to pick up, but it's difficult, very, very difficult.

First of all they're brought up in this country, and they have their own families now. They have their church activities, school activities. Whereas in the organization like ours, we do not have that kind of activity to offer to the young people, to attract them. Unless we got some very innovative programs, it's tough.

Each year we sponsor a picnic, which attracts a lot of young people. We started a very good scholarship program where we can encourage the young people to be good students and we award them some money each year. Now, through that kind of participation, they seem to know there is a Yee Association here and they start taking interest in this thing. Maybe this kind of program will eventually be able to generate some interest among the young people. Besides, we've got some young leaders now, so they may be able to do something about that.

James Yee worked at the Boeing Company for many years as the Senior Principle Engineer. He retired in 1991. Yee is still active in the Yee Association and was recently given the esteemed National Yee Association title of "Grand Advisor." With this title, he is able to travel to many conventions and events courtesy of this national association, what he considers as his "retirement benefits." He and his wife have five children and 19 grandchildren.

George K. Yee

Born November 15, 1906, Toisan District, Kwangtung Province, China
Died November 7, 1991, Seattle, Washington

I believe that there will always be discrimination in this country. Immigration discrimination was very prevalent in the early years – that is why many Chinese could not bring their families over. The years after Kennedy have been much better. There is more mobility for Asians now and the immigration laws allow many more Chinese to enter the U.S.

The Chinese community is more open now than before. We don't just rely on ourselves to resolve problems. This is a sign of progress. Chinese are more involved with politics – knowing that political power is important if we want to have our voice heard. With better education and less discrimination, young Chinese have more opportunities than the old-timers, but they still have to work hard and prove themselves in order to succeed. Young people, while they should assimilate with the main society, should not disregard their Chinese roots. With better education and command of the English language and being accepted more by whites, they should be able to lead a better life than their parents.

George Yee was a partner in the Wah Young Company from 1953 until his retirement in the late 1980s. He held leadership positions in the Chong Wa Benevolent Association, Chinatown Chamber of Commerce and the Yee Family Association. Photo early 1950s.

After serving as a radio operator in the Army during World War II, Warren Chan used the G.I. Bill to go to law school at the University of Washington. He is the first Chinese American to become a practicing attorney in Seattle. In 1968, he became the first Chinese American elected as judge in Washington state.

陳文華

Warren Chan

Born December 29, 1922, San Francisco, California

When I graduated from law school, the dean took me aside and said, "Warren, what do you want to do?" I said, "Practice law." He said, "What I think you ought to do is go see Judge Steinert." He headed the OPA – the Office of Price Administration. During and after World War II, everything was controlled: prices, rents and salaries. I didn't see any future in that, so I rejected it. He said, "You need it." He never told me the real reason.

When I started looking for a job in the law firms, I realized what the dean of the law school had in mind. I think I was interviewed by three different law firms and never received any kind of encouragement. They never said "yes" or "no" or anything. I believe I graduated fourth in my class in law school. I had been on the Law Review. I had spent a year in the Supreme Court as a law clerk. It was discouraging to see many of my classmates – "C" students – getting hired, and here I was – fourth in the class – and I had a terrible time getting a job.

By then, I had decided that the best thing for me to do was just try to get some office space, handle cases for some lawyer in payment for rent, and get some experience that way. That's how I started.

I ran for Superior Court judge in 1968. I filed against some old judge in whom the lawyers just really had no confidence. As I heard it, there were cases waiting, and he'd be sitting in his chambers, twiddling his thumbs, because none of the lawyers wanted him as the judge. They'd sign and take an affidavit, and the clerk, to avoid having these affidavits filed against the judge, would just not send him any cases. When I announced, there were a number of lawyers who were willing to support me.

Trial work has the real-life drama of the trial and witnesses in the courtroom. I also served as judge pro tem on the Supreme Court. As between the two, I've always said that being a trial judge is fun work.

I don't think my values have changed, but I think, like so many individuals, after one sees the same thing over and over and over again, nothing sounds fresh or new. In other words, somebody comes up and says, "I didn't really have the drugs. It was planted on me by an officer." I've heard it so many times, and it doesn't have the ring of truth. It isn't given that good strong consideration that perhaps it's entitled.

I think that one of the very important things is that the Chinese community has become more politicized. It's very aware now of political matters, and I'd like to think that I had a hand in it, first by supporting candidates when I was much younger, and secondly, by running for office myself and encouraging others to run for office.

The Chinese community isn't where it was years ago when all of the contact with the Caucasian world was through representatives. The tongs and the family associations had a member whom they called *choot-fan*. That was the person who dealt with lawyers. If somebody needed a lawyer, the *choot-fan* would get a lawyer. In other areas, the individual was the representative for the Chinese organization or its members. Many of the Chinese are in the mainstream now, whereas 30 years ago, they were not.

In 1973, Liem Tuai ran for Mayor of Seattle. Although he was unsuccessful, he was the first Asian American to seek that position. After 19 years of service as a King County Superior Court judge, he retired and continued to serve as a legal advocate for the community.

伍兆濂

Liem Eng Tuai

Born December 2, 1925, Port Townsend, Washington
Died March 2, 2003, Seattle, Washington

I don't know how your family was, but my parents never showed any affection. I came back after I was in the service, and the first thing my mother says is, "Are you hungry?" That's their way of showing affection. None of the hugging and this type of thing. It just wasn't done.

I went into law because I felt my family got screwed by a lawyer when my father died. It turned out not to be true. That kind of led me to the path of saying, "These guys aren't going to screw us anymore." It was a little bit of a racial thing.

I was appointed to the City Council in May of 1969. At the time, I thought it was a part-time job. That was the only reason I took it. They were only making $12,000 in those days. I thought I could keep going with my law practice, but I soon found out that I just couldn't do it.

We had all kinds of folks there on the City Council. They were going in every which direction. I was trying to pull together a group of us so that we could get some work passed rather than fight over it. Compromise among ourselves. This is the days before the open meetings and the full disclosure laws. Five of us would get together for lunch or dinner or meet on Saturday afternoon and try to get something that we could all agree upon and then move on from there. And we did. This was the time we had the Model Cities Program money. We had the War Against Poverty money coming in, and there were a lot of programs that we had to go through, approve and fund.

I quit when I ran for Mayor. I've just never felt comfortable sitting down and compromising all the time. I just wanted to do something – whether it was right or wrong or indifferent – and not sit around at the table and say, "All right, you take 10 of these and I'll take 10 of those, and we'll shift and we'll end up in the middle." In politics, I never felt comfortable being a member of a legislative body as such.

We spent, I think, $130,000 on the campaign and none of it came from my pocket. In those days, $100,000 was a hell of a lot of money. What made me feel good was all these people coming out of the woodwork that wanted to help. I remember the Italian dinners we had. Just a tremendous outpouring. These people – most of them I didn't know and probably will never see again – came down and worked at the headquarters, and they did all these things it takes to run a campaign. Win, lose or draw, I thought that was just great.

I was appointed to the bench in 1977 by Governor Dixy Lee Ray and that's what I wanted to do, so it's ended up where I wanted to end up. I've enjoyed my tenure on the bench. I can say that without hesitation. I've attained some level of intellectual achievement by being there and being able to make decisions. Of course, obviously, when you make a decision, half of the people that have been in your court aren't going to be happy, which is the nature of the beast. I think I put in the time, I think I put in the effort, and I think I'm knowledgeable enough to make those decisions.

Calvin Fung

Born November 5, 1924, San Francisco, California

My father was a U.S. immigration officer. He acted as the interpreter, handling papers for those immigrants that came over. He was a very well-to-do man. I don't recall anything that the family lacked, even during the Depression. He was very well respected in Chinatown. In 1938, the government transferred my father to Seattle.

The only time I was close to my father was when Jeni and I got married. When we got married, my dad was retired. He was a diabetic with failing health. Jeni was taking care of him. He got to know us and he became a little freer. You know, you never ask personal questions about the things you want to really know. It was a short period we got to know him. It's too bad – last few years. I would have asked him where he was born, more about his family, his education, how he got over here, the jobs that he had, how he met my mother and Mother's background.

The thing I am proud about with our girls, if anything, is that they have a lot of respect for Jeni. They call her all the time, they ask her to go out and do things. That makes me feel good. That's not to say they don't have respect for their dad, but that's what I see. I think Jeni and I have tried to instill with the girls love for their parents, and I've always told the girls the bottom line is that if anything happens to me, that's the number one thing – take care of your mother.

I think the big difference in our generation is that we moved to the suburbs. Our kids found few Chinese friends. Their association was with Caucasians. I think when you bring them up on the outskirts, they miss a lot of opportunities for meeting more Chinese friends and learning more about their culture. I think as far as their culture goes, it will diminish and not have the same meanings that were taught them.

Cal Fung earned a degree in sociology at Seattle University in 1951. He worked as a purchaser for the Boeing Company from 1958 to 1989. Since his retirement, he has been an active volunteer for the Kin On Nursing Home and the Chinese American veterans' group, the Cathay Post #186 of the American Legion.

Allan Fay Wong

Born October 9, 1917, Toisan District, Kwangtung Province, China
Died June 25, 2003, Seattle, Washingto

They don't consider us American. The Chinese are all just like a group living within the city, but they aren't really social with Americans. They don't seem to want to get really close to us. They come to the store for the business all right, but they are just very distant. Some even call me foreigner. Most of them, they're nice enough. They're very correct. They didn't do anything to hurt us, nothing like that, but you know you are different. That's all. I feel more proud to be Chinese now. We seem to be doing so well now. We seem able to obtain more equality. I'm very happy right now because I see my grandchildren or my children and what they're able to do. I see my grandchildren and I'm very pleased with myself.

During World War II, Allan Fay Wong served in the U.S. Army where he was a Japanese language interpreter. Wong later operated Summit Grocery on Capitol Hill for 31 years before working as produce manager at the Uwajimaya store in Chinatown. He and his wife raised five children.

Ruth Jung Chinn

Born in Los Angeles, California

My father, when he came over to America, said the Chinese must be organized. "If you're not organized, if you don't get your life together, you'll always be looked down upon." He gathered all his family, his relatives all together – from Chinatown, everywhere, out in the suburbs – and before he passed away, he took a whole bundle of sticks and tied the whole bundle together. He said, "Try and break it." My brother couldn't break it. I couldn't break it. Nobody could break it.

He said, "I'll take one stick. See if anybody can break it." Oh, we broke it so easily! "That's how it is," he said. "You stick together as a family, nobody can break you. But if you go out one by one,

Ruth Jung Chinn and her husband, Robert, opened the United Savings and Loan Bank in 1960 as the first Asian American-owned savings and loan institution in the United States. In 1966, she started the Jade Guild, a Chinese American women's service organization. After her husband passed away in 1984, she and her daughter, Karen, took on the task of fulfilling his dream of building a recreational and cultural center in Chinatown. That dream became a reality when the Asian Resource Center opened in 1994.

and don't take care of each other, you're going to all die down the vine."

It was Depression and there were no jobs. My husband didn't have a job. Luckily, I got a job as athletic director for Chinatown under the Collins Field Playhouse Recreation. I was given a territory and Chong Wa was the play field. At that time, the men running Chong Wa were not receptive to the idea of having games in the auditorium, so the Parks Department rented a little hall across from Chong Wa and there we did our crafts and games and activities. We used Chong Wa to put on plays, which they allowed us to do just once.

The men's ideas were not progressive for the time, so a bunch of us women asked all the women who could support us to get some of the women on the board of Chong Wa. It was very hard. We asked the women to come and vote us in because we need that vote to get in – the men are not going to vote for us. The men didn't like it. They didn't want women. Women had never served on it. We were the first ones in the whole United States that got women into the Chong Wa board, so that we can have a say in what goes on in the community.

We started reforms in Chong Wa. We started to have parades and queen contests under Chong Wa. We got recreation equipment for the Chinese school. I set up Chinese conversation class for the young children who haven't got the time to come every day to Chinese school. I taught citizenship and English to get many people to pass that citizenship test.

I thought that our community could be much stronger if we had a Chinese women's club. We thought that "jade" is the most precious stone of China and "guild" would be all the women together, so it was named Jade Guild. From 15 to 16 charter members, we are now about almost a hundred members and we're celebrating our 25th anniversary.

We have two daughters and one son. I raised them according to how my parents raised me. I had very good parents. They gave me the culture. You know when you raise a family, you just don't let them do whatever they want. You got to sit with them and teach them that there's some other things to learn when you're young. That is music, art – appreciate those things and learn your culture and some of the traditions and customs and family respect. It takes time to do these things.

There's an old saying that the old possess a wealth of wisdom and experience; the new are full of vitality and drive. It is hoped that the elders of our community will continue to guide the young, and the young to respect and learn from the elders. This is not only tradition, but also, in and of itself, a way of life, an infallible road to progress. That's what the link is. When my children ask me, "Why do we have to do this, Mother?" I say, "Because we have the experience and the wisdom. You have the youth and vitality. We've got to combine the two. I've got to teach you, and you use it to go out and progress."

The First Arrivals: 1860 - 1880

If gold had not been discovered in California and if living conditions had been better in Southeast China, the Chinese might not have flocked to America. But gold was discovered at a California sawmill in 1848 and the gold fever spread across the Pacific Ocean, carried to China by Chinese merchants in San Francisco. The news spread to villages in Kwangtung Province and soon, many people journeyed to *Gim San* or Gold Mountain, the Chinese name for America. The Chinese who journeyed overseas overwhelmingly came from two provinces, Kwangtung and Fukien. Two nearby seaports – Hong Kong and Canton – attracted trade ships from the West. These ships provided a ready means of travel for the Chinese sojourners.

Many of the early immigrants came from the villages in Toisan District, on a delta at the mouth of the Pearl River. Toisan translates as "elevated mountain," an apt description of the area. For generations, peasants there, living by basic Confucian values, struggled to eke out an existence from the arid, mountainous soil.

In 1842, China lost the Opium War to Great Britain. With defeat, China not only lost its struggle to outlaw the shipment of opium into China, it was also forced to open its ports to trade with the West. Much of the countryside lay in ruins, and peasants had to contend with ruthless landlords and famine. Heavy floods in the Pearl River Delta made conditions worse.

China's political system, based on absolute rule by the Chinese emperor, was nearly uprooted during the Taiping Rebellion. The revolt, which began in 1851, was an unsuccessful 13-year peasant uprising in Southeast China. Meanwhile, the increasing demand for cheap labor on America's western frontier prompted capitalists and their agents to recruit Chinese peasants to work overseas.

By 1880, more than 300,000 Chinese came to the United States, many of them young men. The Chinese came here expecting to work hard and take risks, but they did not expect the acute hatred, cruelty and

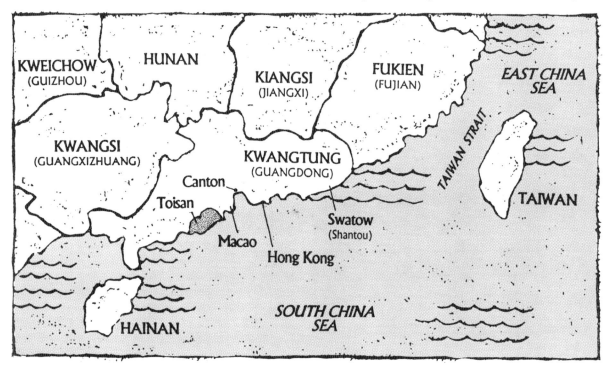

Chinese from Toisan District in Kwangtung Province in Southeast China were the first Chinese immigrants to the U.S. (Illustration by Michelle Kumata)

violence they ultimately encountered. They learned that the *bok guey* or "white devil" was for real. At the time of the 1882 Chinese Exclusion Act – which barred further entry of Chinese laborers – over half of those who emigrated to America returned to China. However, other Chinese continued to make their way to the United States, keeping alive the Chinese presence. They found jobs, established roots, endured discrimination and, when the laws changed, built strong family and community structures.

The first group of Chinese to come to the Pacific Northwest arrived in 1789 as part of the crew of Captain John Meares. They landed on Nootka Sound on Vancouver Island. It is speculated that they may have intermarried with Native Americans. Other Chinese joined the crews of British ships that came to the Northwest as part of the Canton trade route. There is no evidence that these crewmen settled here.

The 1850 census showed that there was one Chinese in Washington Territory. He was listed as "Ah-Long," a servant to Captain Rufus Ingles at Vancouver Barracks in Clark County. There is no record of what happened to him.

Ten years later, there was only one Chinese recorded in the Territorial census. It was probably Chin Chun Hock, who arrived in Seattle in 1860. Chin, 16, came from San Francisco to work as a houseboy.

When Chin arrived, Seattle was still undeveloped. There were only 300 residents – including Native Americans – in what is now King County. Much of Seattle was covered with virgin forests and tidelands. Henry Yesler had recently built the first steam sawmill in Puget Sound in present-day Pioneer Square, on what is now Occidental Avenue.

Chin must have been lonely for the company of his fellow countrymen. In the 1860s, there were only a few Chinese west of the Cascade Mountains. Some Chinese were cooks or laundrymen at the lumber mills of Port Madison, Port Blakely and Port Gamble. Others like Chin worked as houseboys.

Most of the Chinese were in eastern Washington Territory. Thousands came from California and British Columbia to work abandoned mines along the Columbia River and its many tributaries. Others ran small businesses and worked as farmers or servants in Spokane and Walla Walla, where Chinese settlements emerged.

In 1868, one year before Seattle was incorporated as a township, Chin Chun Hock began a general merchandising store called the Wa Chong Company. The business opened next to the tide flat land just south of Yesler's mill. Chin once remarked that he shot wild ducks on the marsh land behind his store, a wooden structure on stilts. The store was a cigar manufacturer, tailor and dealer in sugar, tea and Chinese goods. Some years later, the company advertised the sale of opium, apparently legal at the time.

Between 1870 and 1890, the development of the railroads spurred enormous growth in industry and population. The acute need for laborers to construct the railroads led to a transcontinental recruitment campaign that reached the distant shores of Europe and Asia.

Hundreds were recruited directly from Hong Kong and China. Other Chinese were contracted from San Francisco and Portland. In 1873, some 300 Chinese from Portland arrived in Olympia to lay steel for the stretch of the Northern Pacific Line from Kalama to Tacoma. Eventually, some 15,000 Chinese were hired to work on the Northern Pacific, which ran from Minneapolis to Tacoma.

By 1876, Seattle's population had swelled to 3,400. The number of Chinese grew to 250. There were an additional 300 Chinese transient laborers in the area. These men worked in the coal mines and hop

Chin Chun Hock, standing fourth from the left with a cane, was the first Chinese in Seattle. He established the Wa Chong Company in 1868. At far left is business partner Woo Gen. (Courtesy of Wing Luke Asian Museum)

farms throughout present-day King County. They also worked in lumber mills and fishing industries in Kitsap County, Bainbridge Island and Mukilteo.

After the introduction of trap fishing on Puget Sound, a heavy demand arose for seasonal laborers during the lucrative salmon runs. Many Chinese laborers were hired, and at the end of each fishing season, they cleaned their long knives, stored their boats and went to Seattle and other towns to gamble and wait for their next jobs.

In Seattle, Chinese worked in small businesses owned and operated by Chinese merchants. These enterprises – small laundries, restaurants and dry goods stores – were patronized by whites and Native Americans as well as Chinese. The Native Americans, in fact, regularly patronized the dry goods stores. Not surprisingly, some Chinese learned Native American sign language and Salish.

Other Chinese worked as vegetable peddlers, selling produce grown near present-day Seattle Center and the Duwamish River. Some worked as domestic servants or cooks. There was even one Chinese who peddled ice cream on a converted wheelbarrow. Others engaged in net fishing on Elliott Bay.

Chinese were contracted to work on construction projects around town such as street cleaning, grading and paving. One of the more difficult projects employing Chinese laborers was the Lake Washington canal project. A crew of Chinese dug a canal from Lake Union, around Queen Anne Hill to Salmon Bay.

Until the mid-1870s, the Chinese section of the city was simply a small base for Chinese businesses and transient laborers. The Chinese quarters evolved into Chinatown – a thriving business and residential area – as increasing numbers of Chinese found work in the city through the Wa Chong Company.

During this period, the Chinese quarters gradually shifted from the Commercial-Mill Street area – near what is now Occidental Avenue – to Washington Street, between Second and Third Avenues. This shift – a distance of only several blocks within present-day Pioneer Square – was led by Chin Chun Hock, who moved his prosperous Wa Chong Company to Third and Washington Street. Soon thereafter, other Chinese merchants began to lease buildings along Washington Street.

According to one early settler, the movement of Chinese into the area brought about such resentment by whites that it resulted in the depreciation of property values and the unnatural growth of the city's business district.

"It is entirely likely that had it not been for those Chinese leases just at that time, business in Seattle would have followed the easier grades of Washington, Main and Jackson Streets, instead of going up the steep hill of First Avenue, which was a high bank on the east side and drop off to the waterfront on the west side," wrote J. Willis Sayres (1936) in his book, *This City of Ours*.

The new Chinese area quickly became congested. "In 1877, Washington Street was Chinese headquarters," wrote historian Clarence Bagley (1927). "On that street, there were 27 Chinese houses in about a half a block….During any alarm of fire, they poured out like rats from a burning house."

Woo Ping (McDonald, 1955), an early Chinese merchant, noted that the early Chinatown near Second and Washington was quite colorful: "The buildings had secret hallways and passages in and under them so intricate in their windings that they were even confusing to the Chinese who entered." Here, Chinese – as well as whites and others – indulged in gambling and opium smoking.

The Chinese who congregated in the early Chinatown must have seemed very curious to outsiders. The men wore queues, silk caps, shirts that hung freely from the shoulder to below the waist and wooden-soled slippers. The few Chinese women typically wore trousers and had tiny bound feet.

The 1879 territorial census for King County probably undercounted the Chinese when it listed just 90 men, seven women and four boys. Missing from the count were the large number of transient laborers.

The 1889 Seattle business directory listed the following Chinese businesses: seven wash houses, two grocers, two physicians (probably herbalists), one cook and one merchant (listed as Wa Chong). Few whites entered laundry work, allowing the Chinese to operate wash houses. All that was needed for this business was a small amount of start-up capital and a willingness to work long hard hours.

The Wa Chong Company was easily the preeminent Chinese institution in town up to the 1900s. Its owner, Chin Chun Hock, was the leading Chinese in the community even though Chin Gee Hee, his one-time partner, became the spokesman for the town's Chinese and had stronger ties to Seattle's leading white citizens.

The Wa Chong Company did everything. The retail store sold general merchandise, silk, tea, opium, firecrackers, furniture, china, herbs, linen, clothing and other goods imported from China via Victoria, B.C. Wholesale goods were provided to Chinese businesses throughout Washington, Idaho and Montana. Large quantities of flour and wheat were shipped to China.

The company's biggest operation, and where Chin gained his prominence, was the contracting of labor. The Wa Chong Company, the only contractor in town, responded to requests from the entire territory for Chinese to work as cooks, laundry workers, houseboys and laborers on the railroads, in hop farms, coal mines, lumber mills, canneries and local street improvement projects. Its bigger contracting jobs included work on the Columbia River, Puget Sound, Northern Pacific Railroad and local street grading projects. "I graded Pike, Union, Washington and Jackson Streets," Chin (*History of Chinese in Seattle*, 1976) once remarked. "At one time, the city owed me $60,000 for six months. I had to sue to recover it."

Chin Chun Hock made a fortune that included substantial real estate holdings. In addition to two buildings he owned on Third Avenue and Washington Street, he also owned a building on Fourth Avenue and South Main Street, where he ran the Wa Chong Company for nearly 20 years before moving it to King Street. The Oak Tin Family Association

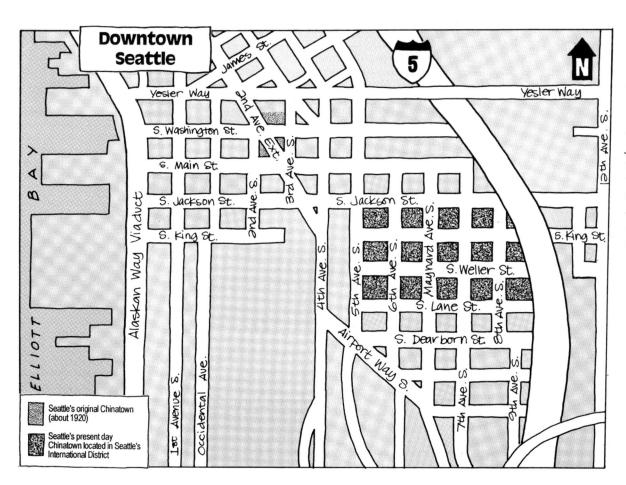

Seattle's original Chinatown was located on Second Avenue and Washington Street. The second Chinatown was built on newly regraded Jackson Street in the early 1900s. By the late 1930s, "Chinatown" was established as a district neighborhood. (Illustration by Michelle Kumata)

(Hall of Brotherhood) began at Fourth and Main Street in space provided by Chin. Chin Chun Hock, if not the most prominent Chinese in the area, was certainly the wealthiest. He was always quick to provide assistance to his fellow countrymen.

When Chin left Seattle in 1900, he took with him millions of dollars and two wives, one a daughter of Chief Sealth. A true entrepreneur, he started a bank and lumber business upon his return to Toisan. Although he told his business partners that he would return to Seattle, he never did. The operations of the company were left to his partners.

The Wa Chong Company was more than just a business. It was the central gathering place for Chinese Americans. It was a community center, post office, labor hall, dormitory, gambling hall and opium den all rolled into one. Nearly all the Chinese who came to town went there to seek food, shelter, work and companionship. Chinese were excluded from most public and private establishments in Seattle except churches, which accepted them on a conditional basis. Religious institutions were more open because they saw an opportunity to spread their gospel and convert and Americanize the "heathen" Chinese.

In 1880, the Reverend Don Quong, a Chinese preacher, took charge of 15 to 20 Chinese parishioners in Seattle. The Methodist preacher held services on Sunday evenings, after the regular church attendees finished their services. It must have been a success because two years later, a school for Chinese children was established at the Methodist Episcopal Church at Fourth Avenue and Columbia Street in downtown Seattle. About 40 children attended the classes, which were taught by two women.

The efforts to convert the Chinese reflected an underlying belief that the Chinese immigrants were products of an unclean, inferior culture. At its worst, this attitude would flare into vicious intolerance when economic conditions worsened and white workers sought to permanently oust Chinese from competition for jobs. By the time of the 1886 anti-Chinese riots in Seattle, there were about 400 Chinese in the city. Many were out of jobs and trying to survive in a depressed economy like everyone else.

The Anti-Chinese Movement: 1880 - 1890

Although many European immigrants were arriving in Washington Territory at the same time as the Chinese, no group – except perhaps the Native Americans – alarmed the white settlers as much as the Chinese. The "Chinese Problem" became a major issue from the time Washington was a territory until after it gained statehood in 1889.

When Washington Territory was created in 1853, legislators immediately adopted a measure to deny Chinese the right to vote, even though there were few, if any, Chinese living in the territory.

By the mid-1860s, territorial legislators passed additional anti-Chinese laws. One law barred Chinese from testifying against whites in court. Another measure, titled, "An Act to Protect Free White Labor Against Competition with Chinese Coolie Labor and to Discourage the Immigration of Chinese in the Territory," resulted in a poll tax levied on every Chinese. The legislators were following the lead established by California lawmakers who had enacted similar measures against its Chinese residents.

During the next decade, however, hostility against the Chinese was not always evident. In railroad construction, for example, whites generally reacted without animosity to the employment of Chinese. According to historian Robert E. Wynne (1978), "The work was so obviously needed and all groups and areas vied with each other to entice a company to build a railroad in their area that they would have welcomed the devil himself had he built a road . . . . The lack of white labor was too evident to cause even the most ardent anti-Chinese to resent their employment on such work." On occasion, the arrival of shiploads of Chinese laborers was greeted by cheers. It signaled economic progress for the area.

The rancorous attitude against the Chinese, however latent at times, was quick to flare up. In Sultan, a small town northeast of Seattle, neither Native Americans nor whites liked them and eventually the few Chinese prospectors there were run off their claims. At work sites, Chinese workers were often physically and verbally abused.

A severe economic downturn in the 1880s meant jobs were scarce. White settlers began to call for the removal of all Chinese from the

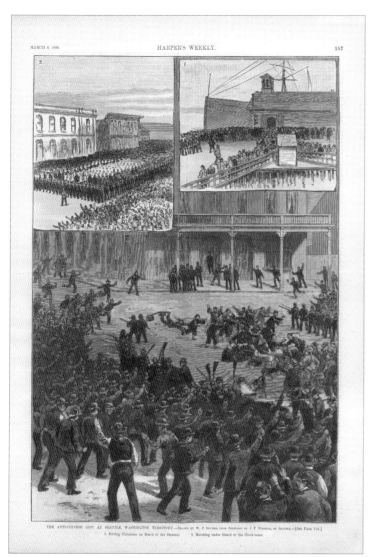

On February 7, 1886, a mob of white workers rounded up all 350 Chinese living in Seattle and attempted to load them onto a boat leaving the city. Two hundred Chinese left on a boat the next morning, but 150 remained stranded at the shore. As police tried to escort the group back to their homes, the mob rioted. This illustration from Harper's Weekly shows the violence against the Chinese in Seattle. (Courtesy of Wing Luke Asian Museum)

territory. The spark that precipitated the anti-Chinese outbreaks in Seattle was the riot of September, 1885 in Rock Springs, Wyoming, where 28 Chinese were murdered and over 500 driven out of town. On the night of September 5th, a group of whites and Native Americans, armed with rifles, ambushed 35 Chinese at a hop farm in Squak Valley (now Issaquah), a few miles east of Seattle, killing three and injuring three. The attackers – five whites and two Native Americans – were acquitted after an eight-day trial. On September 19th, the Chinese were driven from the coal mining town of Black Diamond, southeast of Seattle. Nine Chinese were injured in that incident. About one week later, another coal mine east of Seattle ousted its Chinese workers. In yet another clash, a party of masked and armed men entered the Franklin Mines and forced the Chinese onto a special train to Seattle. Similar occurrences were reported in Newcastle and Renton. In all these incidents, no one was brought to trial.

The anti-Chinese forces in Seattle quickly split into two groups. One group, led by labor unions and laborers, favored the direct and immediate removal of the Chinese from the city. The second group – called the "Law and Order" group – was comprised of businessmen and other civic leaders who favored a more orderly process of removal through legislative action. Both groups agreed that the Chinese should be removed. They simply disagreed over tactics.

On Sunday morning, February 7, 1886, following a meeting of the anti-Chinese direct action group the night before, an appointed committee and their followers invaded the Chinese quarters to notify the Chinese they were leaving that afternoon on the steamer, Queen of the Pacific. Most of the 350 Chinese were forced on wagons, hauled to the dock and loaded onto the steamer. The incident prompted Territorial Governor Squire to proclaim a state of insurrection, declare martial law, suspend the writ of habeas corpus and request the intervention of federal troops.

When the next steamer arrived on February 14, 1886, another 110 Chinese boarded. The remaining Chinese were scheduled to leave on the following steamer. One week later, civil law was restored, but it was not until July that the federal troops left. By that time, there were only a handful of Chinese merchants and domestic servants remaining in the city.

Establishing a Permanent Settlement: 1890 - 1910

The anti-Chinese riots were not enough to deter the civic and financial aspirations of one Chinese American, Chin Gee Hee. Chin had been a spokesman for the Chinese during this ordeal. As a partner in the Wa Chong Company, he refused to leave until debts due to his company were collected. With the help of Judge Thomas Burke and the city's business and political establishments, the well-connected Chin and his family were among the few Chinese who stayed in Seattle.

Chin Gee Hee was only a teenager when he arrived in San Francisco in 1862. After a stint at railroad work, he came to Port Gamble to work. There were only a few other Chinese at the sawmill, one of the largest in the world at that time. There, he washed clothes. Anticipating a long stay, he sent for a wife from China, who became a cook at the mill.

A quick learner and a natural talker who was knowledgeable and conversant on current events, he became fluent in English and Salish. He made many friends. At the urging of one-time Seattle mayor and lumber mill owner Henry Yesler, Chin and his wife moved to Seattle in 1873. He became a junior partner in the Wa Chong Company at the invitation of Chin Chun Hock, both of whom were from Look-Choon Village in Toisan.

Labor contracting quickly became Chin Gee Hee's specialty. It was a job that perfectly complimented his language skills, bicultural knowledge, outgoing personality and financial aspirations. He established the Wa Chong Company as the leading Chinese labor contractor in Washington Territory. The Wa Chong Company steadily prospered for over a decade.

But the pressures and ordeal of the anti-Chinese climate and the lingering business tension between Chin Gee Hee and Chin Chun Hock, the founder of the Wa Chong Company, became too much. In 1887, they agreed to go their separate ways.

One year later, Chin Gee Hee started the Quong Tuck Company, also a general merchandise store that imported and exported goods and contracted labor.

After the anti-Chinese riot, Chin Gee Hee watched a gradual return of his countrymen to Seattle from his newly-built Quong Tuck building at Second Avenue and Washington Street. His elegant structure was the first brick building constructed in the city after the Great Seattle Fire of 1889, which leveled the downtown area. Meanwhile, Chin Chun Hock constructed a building right around the corner on Second Avenue. The Second Avenue and Washington Street area also had three Chinese restaurants, eight laundries, a grocery and four general merchandise stores. These establishments formed the core of Seattle's early Chinatown.

Chinatown was mostly a bachelor society. Before 1882, Chinese women, bound by tradition, stayed home in China. After 1882, Chinese laborers in America were bound by a provision of the Chinese Exclusion Act which barred them from bringing over wives. Roughly a third of the Chinese men were married, but there were very few families and women in Seattle.

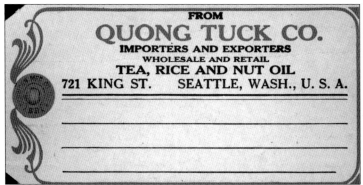

Businesses such as the Wa Chong and Quong Tuck companies specialized in international trade between Seattle and East Asia, providing Chinese goods for the community. (Courtesy of Wing Luke Asian Museum)

The 400 to 500 Chinese in the city lived in near seclusion from other Seattleites. They occupied small rooms above storefronts on Washington Street, from Second to Fifth Avenues. After working long hours, they found respite in gambling and storytelling, then they packed into their rooms to sleep at the end of the day.

With the arrival of the Nippon Yusen Kaisha steamship line to Seattle, Chinese businesses experienced a modest surge in growth. The new steamship line not only provided direct passenger service to Asia, it also enabled Chinese businesses to get direct shipments from China. Chinese stores in Seattle began to stock their shelves with dried ducks, sweet-smelling roots, bamboo bales, herbs, smoked meat, tea and an assortment of packaged goods. They became wholesale suppliers of Chinese goods to restaurants, general stores and work camps in the state and as far away as Alaska, Idaho and Montana.

Seattle witnessed one of its greatest periods of economic expansion during the decade of the 1890s – nearly doubling its population. At the same time, however, the Chinese net population increased by one person. Chinese laborers were not in great demand. Although Chinese continued to arrive in the United States – including some that were smuggled over the Canadian border – other Chinese left America for good, returning home to China.

The situation looked so bleak that Chin Gee Hee, in an interview with the *Seattle Post-Intelligencer* ("By and By, No More Chinese" 1899), predicted there would be no Chinese left in the city in 10 to 12 years. His prediction, of course, did not come true. Chin failed to take into account the exploding demand for seasonal laborers in the canneries on Puget Sound and in Alaska. Thousands of Chinese also worked in canneries along the Columbia River, where the Northwest cannery industry began in 1871.

Chinese contractors recruited and hired Chinese laborers, competing against one another for contracts. They were typically responsible for supervising, providing food for and paying crews at the end of the season. Cannery work usually ran from April through September.

The work was hard. Once the salmon was unloaded, the Chinese cannery workers gutted, cleaned and canned them in containers hammered into shape over iron cylinders. Then, they soldered the cans and cooked the fish. Average pay was about $50 per month.

At its peak in 1889, there were 39 canneries on the Columbia River. But as the salmon runs slowed on the Columbia, the number of canneries there decreased and began sprouting on the upper Puget Sound in Mukilteo, Anacortes, Bellingham, Blaine, Port Blakely and Alaska. In a few years, the fishing industry became one of the state's most prosperous enterprises, generating revenues in excess of $5.5 million.

Chinese were hired in great numbers as canneries emerged along Puget Sound. Over 2,000 arrived annually by boat from Portland and San

Chin Gee Hee built the first brick building in Seattle after the Great Seattle Fire of 1889. The structure, located at Second Avenue and Washington Street, housed the Quong Tuck Company, a general store that served as the headquarters for his labor contracting operation. (Courtesy of Wing Luke Asian Museum)

Francisco. On Bellingham Bay, as elsewhere, a "China House" was built with a kitchen, dining room, storeroom, store and living quarters for 200 Chinese. At the end of the cannery season, more and more of the men chose to go to Seattle, where they found more plentiful and cheaper housing than in Portland or San Francisco.

Almost overnight, more Chinese businesses appeared. Chinatown grew to three blocks on Washington Street and two side streets. Stores were on the street level of multi-story buildings and rooms for lodging were upstairs. The Wa Chong Company, Quong Tuck Company and Mark Ten Suie – the big three – were the largest, oldest and most prosperous Chinese businesses at the turn of the century. In addition to the big three, Chinatown was the site of the Hop Sing Tong "joss house" and over 20 other businesses, including tailor and curio shops that catered exclusively to non-Chinese.

In 1902, the "Iron Chink" appeared in the canneries. It was a complicated machine that was supposed to butcher fish and replace the Chinese workers. The "Iron Chink" mechanized some tasks, but it didn't eliminate the Chinese. Workers were still needed to operate the machines. Cannery labor contractors like Chin Gee Hee, Woo Gen, Mark Ten Suie, Mar Dong, Chin Seay, Goon Dip and others made huge profits while dominating the recruitment of cannery workers. The workforce also included Japanese and Filipinos. The canneries remained a major source of employment for Chinese until the 1930s, when the recruitment of workers by labor contractors was supplanted by unions.

The growth of the Chinese community and the spurt in his business were good for Chin Gee Hee. In 1905, he returned to China to fulfill his dream of building a railroad in his native Toisan.

"The Chinese population of the city of Seattle can truthfully be classified as among the pioneer builders of the great Pacific Northwest," wrote Lew G. Kay (1909), the first Chinese to graduate from the University of Washington, in an article in *The Coast Magazine*. "Some of them have returned to their fatherland to assist in the industrial and commercial revolution which will greatly increase the trade in the Orient and thus make the Pacific Ocean as the main channel of the world's commerce. This was recently exemplified by the placing of large shipments of modern machinery to local firms, through the influence of former Chinese merchants of Seattle who have returned to China as financial and industrial leaders."

Kay's article appeared in the same year as the Alaska-Yukon-Pacific Exposition, a world's fair held on site of the present University of Washington campus. Businessman Goon Dip arrived in Seattle from Portland in 1908 to organize efforts to create a Chinese pavilion for the exhibition. Another Chinese contractor, Ah King, president of the King Chong Lung Company, helped finance the pavilion, and nearly every Chinese in the city contributed $4 to the undertaking.

Coincidentally, in 1909, Seattle was completing work on the Jackson Street Regrade Project, a major engineering feat which involved filling in Jackson and King Streets with dirt and converting tide flat land into an area for development. The timing of the project was perfect for the Chinese, whose numbers doubled to 900 during the decade. Washington Street was becoming too congested. After completion of the regrade project, Chinese expanded their settlement to what is now the present Chinatown.

After achieving success as a labor contractor, Chin Gee Hee returned to Toisan to fulfill his dream of building a railroad. His supporters included Judge Thomas Burke and other Seattle leaders. Chin is pictured here in his office. (Courtesy of Wing Luke Asian Museum)

The first Chinese buildings constructed on King Street were the Hip Sing Tong building on the northeast corner of Eighth and King Street and two huge buildings between Seventh and Eighth Avenues on the south side. They were built in 1910. A Chinese group, the Kong Yick

Investment Company, was established for the sole purpose of constructing the latter two buildings. Chinese throughout the Northwest bought shares to finance the projects. No bank financing was involved. Chinese ignored banks and vice-versa.

The Wa Chong Company and Quong Tuck Company immediately moved into the Kong Yick buildings. The Yuen Long Company and Yick Fung & Company, an importer-exporter and agent for the Blue Funnel steamship line, followed shortly thereafter. These were the first Chinese businesses on King Street. One of the Kong Yick buildings later housed the elaborate King Fur Café and the Gee How Oak Tin Family Association, the largest Chinese family association in the state.

The following year, 1911, Goon Dip built the Milwaukee Hotel, an elegant structure on Seventh Avenue and King Street. That same year, the Eastern Hotel was built on Maynard Avenue between King and Weller Streets, supposedly for the Wa Chong Company. In 1916, the Bing Kung Tong constructed its building on King Street across from the Kong Yick buildings and, in 1920, a Chinese association built the Republic Hotel on Seventh Avenue between Jackson and King Streets.

By 1925, King Street had become the core of the new Chinatown. The old Chinatown on Washington Street had withered to little more than a few lottery and gambling houses.

The new Chinatown on King Street was only a few blocks southeast of the old Chinatown and right next to the Japanese settlement, which extended from Second to 12th Avenue, between Yesler and Jackson Streets. There were also a number of Italian and African American establishments throughout the area and, later, Filipino businesses. Rainier Power and Heat Company, which owned seven or eight large pieces of property was, by far, the largest single property owner in the area.

One of the earliest outside visitors to the new Chinatown was Dr. Sun Yat-Sen, who led the overthrow of the Manchu Dynasty. Sun, the founder and first president of the Republic of China, arrived in Seattle in September, 1911 just one month before the Manchus were overthrown. Sun had garnered great support from the overseas Chinese, who contributed generously to his revolutionary movement.

Sun's fundraising event, supposedly shrouded in secrecy, was attended by 150 people. Dinner was held at the King Fur Café, on the second floor of the newly built Kong Yick building. After dinner, Sun (Reddin, 1972) gave an one-hour speech on the third floor, the temporary location of the Gee How Oak Tin Family Association. He told a 13-year-old boy after his talk: "There are 400 million people in China, but if I had just one million like you, I know we would have a successful revolution and, perhaps, a united China."

Chinese laborers butchered fish in canneries along the Columbia River, on Puget Sound and in Alaska. (Photo by Anders B. Wilse. Courtesy of Museum of History and Industry, Seattle)

In 1910, the Kong Yick Investment Company erected this building on King Street in the heart of the new Chinatown. (Courtesy of Wing Luke Asian Museum)

From Sojourners to Immigrants: 1910 - 1941

In the early 1900s, nothing was more important to the Chinese than teaching Chinese language and culture to the young. Young people, ages five to 18, attended Chinese school five days a week after public school and on Saturdays. Chinese school was also held through the summer. The curriculum included Chinese history, the teachings of Confucius and Chinese language.

Chinese school was held on the first floor of a two-story building on 12th Avenue and Yesler Way, the same site as the Honorary Chinese Consulate's office. Chin Chun Hock and later, Goon Dip, paid most of the school's operating expenses. Parents of students also covered part of the expenses. For a short period before the overthrow of the Manchu Dynasty in 1911, the Chinese imperial government sent teachers to the United States and matched school funds raised by local merchants. Eventually, the school was supported through funds raised by the Chong Wa Benevolent Association, the major umbrella organization of the Chinese family associations and tongs in Washington state.

The all-boys school had no more than 15 students when it began around the turn of the century. By 1909, enrollment gradually increased to 42 when a Chinese female editor from San Francisco chastised school trustees for not allowing girls to attend. Enrollment did not increase substantially despite the admission of girls. In 1930, when the school relocated to the newly built Chong Wa Benevolent Association on Seventh Avenue and Weller Street, enrollment reached 100 and peaked at 275 during World War II. The size of Chinese school enrollment reflected the small number of Chinese families in the city. There were only a handful of families in 1900 and the number increased slowly until the 1940s.

The Chinese formed a small, isolated community, essentially comprised of aging single men who were more like sojourners in orientation than immigrants. Though they lived most of their lives in America, they only thought of returning to China in their old age to live out their remaining years.

In 1910, there were 860 males and 72 females in Seattle – a ratio of 13 to one. Ten years later, there were 1,180 males and 181 females. In 1930, there were 1,000 males to 350 females and in 1940, 1,350 males to 450 females. Not until the 1970 census did the ratio of males to females begin to even out.

Chinese youngsters prepare for Chinese school, 1940s. (Courtesy of Paul Mar)

Clearly, the 1882 Chinese Exclusion Act and subsequent exclusionary laws severely impeded the growth of families. It took decades for a significant second generation to emerge. The Chinese, however, still managed to come to America through two methods.

First, many falsely claimed American citizenship. After the 1906 San Francisco fire destroyed city records, Chinese began claiming America as their birthplace – making them automatic citizens. If these "American-born citizens" returned home to China, they invariably reported the birth of sons. Years later, when these sons – some real and some "paper" impostors – came of age, they were permitted by birthright to join their fathers in America.

Second, some Chinese immigrants claimed they were merchants, a group exempt from the exclusion laws. To earn that status, they bought partnerships in Chinese American businesses. These businesses frequently had a large number of partners, only a small number of whom actually ran the business.

In 1910, the median age of Chinese in Washington state was 45. Ten years later, it was 42. The median age of Chinese in Seattle could not have been much different. It was clearly a community of mostly older men who had come to Seattle for work. Many had been in the United States for a long time, but had yet to achieve enough wealth to return. Others, despite hardships here, felt that opportunities and living conditions were better in America than in the villages from which they came.

Except for seasonal work in the canneries of Alaska and Bellingham, outside work in the white society was almost non-existent for the Chinese. They were hamstrung by their inability to speak English, lack of skills, insufficient education and discrimination. Typically, Chinese bachelors worked long hours at Chinese restaurants, import-export stores, general merchandise stores, curio shops, hotels, gambling houses, canneries or hand laundries. In 1920, there were over 30 Chinese hand laundries in the city, most located outside of Chinatown in the downtown area. Several were located on Capitol Hill.

Among the small number of women in the community, there is no greater story of strength and courage than that of Dong Oy and her daughter, Margaret. Dong Oy was the wife of Chin Lem, son of Chin Gee Hee. Chin Gee Hee wanted a grandson as heir to his fortune. Disappointed at the birth of a girl, he ordered the young family to return to Toisan. There, Chin Lem deserted his family and went off to find a new wife at the insistence of his father. After a year, Dong Oy fled with her daughter to her mother's house in Hong Kong. Chin Lem found them and told Dong Oy to go to authorities and obtain a birth certificate for a two-month-old boy he bought as their son. Then, he said, they could all leave for Seattle. But, after she obtained the birth certificate and withdrew $700 of the $900 she had at a Shanghai bank for Chin Lem to purchase tickets, he disappeared with the money and left her again.

For months, Dong Oy searched for her husband to no avail. In desperation, she pawned her jewelry to get herself and her daughter to Seattle. Simultaneously, police officers issued Dong Oy a warrant for falsely swearing to the boy's birth certificate. When she appeared in court, Chin Gee Hee and his relatives were there. After Dong Oy's mother and friends raised $250 bail for her release, Chin Lem convinced her to jump bail and return to Toisan. There, Chin Lem deserted her for the last time.

Chin Gee Hee ordered all seaports and railroad stations watched, but by disguising themselves, Dong Oy and Margaret evaded guards and reached Hong Kong. After two months of hiding, they boarded a steamer to Shanghai, then to Yokohama, where Dong Oy sold the last of her jewelry for $80 passage on the S.S. Empress of India. They arrived in Seattle in April, 1909 when Margaret was 12 years old.

Margaret Chin, pictured in the 1920s, was the first Chinese woman to attend the University of Washington. Her husband, Sam Chin, was the first Chinese architect in the state. (Courtesy of Wing Luke Asian Museum)

In Chinatown, Dong Oy took care of babies for other families and sewed for a living. In 1917, while Margaret was in her second year at the University of Washington, they started a Chinese tearoom on 14th Avenue Northeast in the University District. Dong Oy was greatly admired in the community.

Margaret later married Sam Chin, the first Chinese licensed architect in the state and the designer of the Chong Wa building. Despite his education and training, Chin never really worked as an architect due to racial discrimination, which prevented most Chinese American college graduates from obtaining employment in their chosen professions.

One of the few Chinese to graduate from college and find work in his trained profession was Helm Kee Chinn. His father, Chinn We-Shing, came to America in the 1860s and worked on the railroads. He later went to Port Blakely, where he worked at a lumber mill and operated a laundry before moving his family to Seattle. Helm Kee Chinn and his brother were among the first Chinese to graduate in engineering from the University of Washington. He went on to earn a master's degree, the first Chinese at the university to do so. Chinn was fortunate to get a job with the Army Corps of Engineers, where he was in charge of building dams in Oregon and Montana.

Chinese, particularly the bachelors, lived in cramped rooms in tong buildings, family associations and Chinatown hotels. The few merchant families lived in hotel units that combined single rooms. Children played in alleys or vacant lots, seldom roaming beyond Chinatown except for school.

Beginning around 1920, some families moved to residential neighborhoods. Helm Kee Chinn and his father purchased two houses, side by side, on 17th Avenue, not far from Chinatown. Several years earlier, Mar Dong, who came from San Francisco in 1907 and quickly established himself as a successful businessman, bought a house on 29th Avenue in what is now the Central District. His family was probably the first Chinese family to move out of Chinatown.

By 1940, about 40 Chinese families had moved into the Central District. At the same time, Chinese also began moving to the north Beacon Hill area. Other areas of the city were closed because covenants restricted the sale of homes to non-whites.

In 1922, a new Chinese Baptist Church was erected in Chinatown on 10th Avenue and King Street to replace the earlier church founded by Baptist missionaries in 1896 at Fifth Avenue and Yesler Way. The church was a magnet for social and religious activities in the community. Virtually every Chinese child in the city attended the Baptist Church Nursery School, where they experienced the first taste of graham crackers and milk.

Some Chinese businesses – such as import-export businesses that supplied Chinese restaurants – were able to survive solely on a Chinese clientele. But most other Chinese businesses – including restaurants, hand laundries and curio shops – relied on a large base of non-Chinese customers.

Charlie Louie came to Seattle from Portland in 1904 and worked at a laundry, then he became head bartender of the Lincoln Hotel. Later, he opened the Tien Heung (Heavenly Flavor), the city's first downtown Chinese restaurant on Third Avenue and Pike Street. His success led him to open other restaurants and a Chinese import-export establishment on King Street.

In 1923, Louie took a bold step and built a Chinese opera house on Seventh Avenue between King and Weller Streets. Despite bringing in

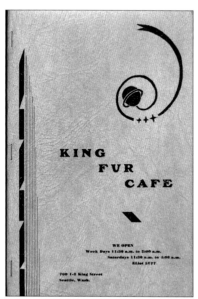

Chinese restaurants such as the King Fur Café, Chinese Garden Restaurant, New Chinatown Café and Twin Dragon Chinese Café opened soon after the new Chinatown had begun development. (Courtesy of Wing Luke Asian Museum)

talent from San Francisco and Hong Kong, he discovered he needed to book prize fights to make the place successful. Finally, in 1929, he converted the opera house into Louie's Chinese Garden, a restaurant with a dance hall. It became one of the city's most popular night spots, attracting many white customers.

In the 1930s, the King Fur Café, Mar's Café, Twin Dragon Café and Danny Woo's New Chinatown Restaurant were all popular Chinatown night spots, attracting both Asian and non-Asian customers. The King Fur, New Chinatown and Louie's Chinese Garden often booked African American jazz musicians.

The first Chinese newspaper in Seattle was *The Chinese Star*, established in 1921. Four individuals worked on the weekly publication, including Willard Jue, who arrived from Portland and was a student at the University of Washington. The newspaper covered news from China as well as the local community and was supported by the Nationalist Chinese government. It ceased publication in 1927, leaving local non-English reading Chinese dependent on Chinese newspapers from Vancouver, B.C. and San Francisco.

In 1929, the Chong Wa Benevolent Association building was constructed next to Louie's Chinese Garden. The two-story building immediately became the pride and focal point of the Chinese community. Dong Shee Chuan (also known as Dong On Long) was the president at the time. The first floor housed classrooms for the Chinese school and the upper floor had a large auditorium with a stage. Dignitaries from all over the United States attended the opening.

Chong Wa was the governing body for all Chinese in Washington state and represented the community to the outside world. In 1931, upon news of Japan's invasion of Manchuria, Chong Wa organized a boycott of Japanese stores in the area. Those who did not participate were ostracized from the community. Through the end of World War II, Chong Wa organized numerous fundraisers to support China's war effort and to assist war victims.

During the Great Depression, Chong Wa regularly distributed food to the needy, even though the Chinese community may not have felt the impact of those times as much as other groups. Chinese had grown accustomed to making do with very little, and many continued to work in the canneries, gambling houses and restaurants.

Adding to the hardship of the Depression was the loss of one of the Chinese community's greatest leaders. In 1933, Goon Dip, the "Merchant Prince" known for his generosity, passed away.

Goon Dip had arrived in Portland in 1876 at the age of 14. He subsequently worked as a general laborer on the railroads in Tacoma and Montana. He returned to Toisan to marry, and upon his return, found himself jobless. However, a sympathetic American woman took him home and convinced her parents to hire Goon as a houseboy. She later taught him English.

The Chong Wa Benevolent Association building opened in 1929. (Courtesy of Wing Luke Asian Museum)

Goon Dip was appointed Honorary Chinese Consul for the Northwest in 1908. (Courtesy of Wing Luke Asian Museum)

He then found employment with Moy Bok-Hin, a millionaire businessman and labor contractor. Goon Dip's English and Chinese language abilities allowed him to quickly assume higher responsibilities since Moy's English was limited.

By 1900, Goon Dip left Moy's business and started his own, a general dry goods store with a hemstitching operation that hired disabled Chinese. He also contracted labor, supplying cooks and cannery workers for the Oregon-Washington Railroad and Navigation Company, which operated riverboats and canneries.

Goon Dip was appointed Honorary Chinese Consul for the Northwest in 1908, replacing his former employer, Moy Bok-Hin. While organizing and working on the Alaska-Yukon-Pacific Exposition, Goon met E.B. Deming, who had just purchased Pacific American Fisheries, a large salmon cannery in south Bellingham. Goon became the sole labor contractor for Deming. Eventually, Pacific American Fisheries became the world's largest salmon cannery, with more than a dozen canneries in Washington and Alaska. Goon Dip became rich.

About 1918, Goon Dip joined Bernard Hirst and C.W. Fries to form the Hirst Chichagof Mine near Juneau, Alaska. Many local Chinese purchased shares in the venture, which turned a profit until the Depression. Taxes and other revenue produced by the mining operation helped keep the Alaska territorial government afloat. As a tribute, a mountain and a river on Chichagof Island were named after Goon Dip. In the community, Goon Dip actively participated in the Kong Yick Investment Company and the Chong Wa Benevolent Association. When he passed away, the city witnessed one of its biggest funerals, and Chinatown mourned for days.

In 1938, the Luck Ngi Musical Society was founded to support the Chinese school, promote Chinese opera and raise funds for other community causes. During World War II, the group put on four or five performances a year at Chong Wa hall. Members honed their skills at 703 1/2 King Street, on the second floor of one of the Kong Yick buildings. There was a small stage, a cabinet for the instruments and small rooms in the back to practice and put on makeup. The members, both China-born and American-born Chinese, came to the Luck Ngi club to practice after work. It was common to hear Chinese music in the wee hours of the morning.

The Luck Ngi Musical Society was founded in 1938 to support the Chinese school, promote Chinese opera and raise funds for the local community as well as war-torn villages in China. (Courtesy of Wing Luke Asian Museum)

Growth of the Community: 1941 - 1965

World War II marked a new chapter in the lives of Chinese Americans. The turning point came when the Japanese bombed Pearl Harbor and the United States became allies with China in the war against Japan.

When twin boys were born to Dick and Annie Wong Chin three months after the United States declared war, *The Seattle Times* (1942) published a photo of the mother with her twins. The headline read, "Chinese Start Right." The caption said, "Training starts early for Chinese children these wartime days," noting that "China" buttons were pinned on the twins' blanket.

For the first time, Chinese were able to enter the mainstream work force and earn decent wages. Labor was badly needed, especially in the defense industry and with companies like Boeing and Todd Shipyard. Those who could speak English – even just a little – signed up as riveters, janitors, mechanic helpers, secretaries or draftsmen. Others were drafted into the armed forces and assigned technical work.

Although many older immigrant bachelors remained at jobs in Chinatown, younger Chinese Americans took over stores and shops left behind by Japanese Americans who were unjustly evacuated to concentration camps during the war.

In 1943, President Franklin D. Roosevelt signed an act sponsored by Washington Senator Warren G. Magnuson – at the urging of local Chinese Americans – repealing the Chinese exclusion laws. Although the new law only established a tiny annual quota of 105 Chinese immigrants to the United States, it allowed Chinese to apply to become naturalized citizens for the first time. Those who became citizens could then apply for their wives to join them. Four years later, Congress amended the War Brides Act, enabling wives of Chinese servicemen to enter the United States on a non-quota basis. Consequently, a number of Chinese servicemen went to China or Hong Kong and returned with wives.

The net result of the passage of the Magnuson and War Brides Acts was the migration of nearly 2,000 Chinese, mostly immigrants, to the state from World War II to 1960. More importantly, the new laws led to a substantial increase in wives and the formation of families. From 1940 to 1960, there were some 1,900 Chinese births in the state, significantly more than the total of the previous 50 years.

The Chinese population in Seattle – according to Calvin Schmid's report (1968), *Nonwhite Races, State of Washington* – increased from 1,781 to 2,650 from 1940 to 1950. In 1960, the number had increased by 65 percent to 4,176. By this time, four-fifths of all Chinese in the state lived in Seattle.

The second generation of Chinese Americans clearly benefited from the events of World War II. According to the 1940 census, just 2.5 percent of the Chinese male work force were professionals or technical workers. Ten years later, it increased to 9.5 percent. By the 1960s, it jumped to 25.5 percent – by far the largest occupational grouping among Chinese males. During this same period, the percentage of Chinese males in the managerial/proprietor occupational grouping fell from 23 percent in 1940 and 25.5 percent in 1950 to 16 percent in 1960. The percentage of waiters and laundry workers also dropped substantially from 1940 to 1960.

Lee Hong Chew, private first class of the 87th Mountain Division, was killed in battle in Italy during World War II. (Courtesy of Ron Chew)

Boy Scout Troop 54, later renamed Troop 254, has helped develop several generations of Chinese American leaders. The troop is pictured in 1930. (Courtesy of Wing Luke Asian Museum)

To say that Chinese were prepared for professional and technical work is an understatement. In 1940, when educational attainment would not have helped Chinese get better jobs, only 2.5 percent of the Chinese in the state were college graduates, compared to six percent for whites. A decade later, the percentage of college graduates among Chinese had jumped to 10.2 percent, surpassing whites, who had eight percent that earned college degrees. By 1960, the percentage of Chinese who had graduated from college had increased to 18 percent, twice as high as whites. "To get a good job," Chinese parents would tell their children, "you have to work twice as hard as the white person and go to college." When attending college meant something in the job market, the Chinese took advantage of it. Despite the dramatic increase in educational attainment, however, the median income of Chinese in the state in 1960 was $2,733, or 69 percent of that for whites.

During the 1940s and '50s, the second generation Chinese Americans were coming into their own. The native-born Chinese – and to a lesser extent, the younger, foreign-born generation – were the product of two cultures. At home, Toisanese was spoken and Confucian thought and behavior were the norm. At school, on the radio, in books and magazines, American values and lifestyles were emphasized.

Cultural values often conflicted. At home, they learned that everything an individual did reflected on the family. They were told to work and study hard, get good grades and attend college so they could do better than their parents. The father's primary role was to support the family. The mother's role was to raise and discipline the children. Everyone lived frugally and delayed personal gratification. Children did as they were told. Being humble was the norm; speaking about your achievements or even about yourself was considered self-centered. Respecting elders, especially relatives – which included all people from the same village and not just those related by marriage or blood – was paramount, as was consideration for others. Those who did not show the right manners were scolded or whipped with the bamboo stick handle of a feather duster.

At American schools, they learned about American values – individualism, democracy and extravagance. They learned about the achievements of western civilization and hardly anything about China or Chinese Americans. They observed their non-Chinese classmates – brash, outspoken, unrestrained – acting very differently from the way they were taught to behave.

While many of their schoolmates were non-Chinese – whites, African Americans, Japanese and Filipinos – their closest friends were usually other Chinese or Japanese. This second generation was a marginal group, feeling the tug of two different cultures, American and Chinese. The second generation developed a new subculture that blended and modified aspects of both cultures.

The second generation's subculture included American cultural institutions set up exclusively for Chinese. In 1923, Boy Scout Troop 54 was established. A Girl Scout Troop was formed in 1940. A Chinese art club that included Fay Chong and Andrew Chinn, both noted watercolor artists, was founded in 1936. After World War II, a Chinese American veterans' group, the Cathay Post #186 of the American Legion, was born, as well as the Miss Chinatown pageant and the Chinatown Chamber of Commerce. Chinese student clubs were formed in high schools and colleges. The group receiving the most acclaim was the Chinese Community Girls' Drill Team, which traveled throughout America and abroad, winning many awards. It was started by restaurateur Ruby Chow in 1951.

Chinese athletic teams had also formed by the 1920s. A Chinese basketball team participated in the Oriental League. Some Chinese excelled in sports, including the Louie brothers, who starred on Garfield High School's football team in the late 1920s; Al Mar, who received All-

The Chinese Community Girls' Drill Team has been a crowd favorite at parades and festivals in Washington state for many years. (Courtesy of Dan Mar)

Coast Honorable Mention as a basketball player for the University of Washington in the 1940s; Milton Lew, a member of the University of Washington tennis team; Ray Soo, All-City and All-State on Garfield's state championship basketball team and later a player for Seattle University; Pete Eng, All-City tackle for Garfield's football team; Jack Eng, number one on Seattle University's tennis team; and Munn Chin, All-City and All-State basketball star for Cleveland High School.

But no one accomplished more in sports than Amy Yee, a tennis champion who probably contributed more to youth tennis in Seattle than any single individual. Born in Cleveland, Ohio, she moved at age six with her family to Vashon Island, where her father had a farm. In high school, she learned to play tennis under Roy Ostrum, former tennis player at Western Washington State College and tennis coach at Vashon High School at the time. A natural athlete, she improved quickly, winning the tri-county high school girls championship in her junior and senior years.

After her marriage in 1944, she moved to Seattle and helped operate the Victory Café on Sixth Avenue and Jackson Street with her husband. She played with a Seattle Chinese tennis team, which competed against Chinese teams from Portland and Vancouver, B.C.

In 1951, she won the first of four Seattle open tournaments, at that time a bigger competition than the state tournament. The following year, she won the Pacific Northwest Championship, and in 1958 and '59, she was the Washington State Women Champion. She also won the Seattle Seafair Singles Championship for 14 years and was the Chinese National Women's Champion for two years. Yee was ranked the number one woman singles player in the Northwest for two years.

In 1959, she was nominated for the *Seattle Post-Intelligencer* "Man of the Year" award. Six years later, her family won the *Seattle Post-Intelligencer* "Sports Family of the Year" award. Both daughters, Joyce and Linda, were Washington State Women's Champions, while her two sons, Gordy and Gary, were nationally-ranked junior players. Gary later went on to become the University of Washington's number one player.

While Amy Yee and the second generation Chinese Americans were making the most of their new-found opportunities, conditions had not improved much for many of the first generation immigrants. Some were able to accumulate enough savings and, with financial help from relatives, started small businesses. These first generation immigrants typically purchased small, family-operated restaurants, grocery stores or laundries in the late 1940s and early '50s. While a family couldn't get rich off of these businesses, they could make enough to survive.

Joe Locke was typical of this group. He came to America on a steamship with his parents when he was eight years old. They arrived in Olympia, where there was already an established Locke clan. He attended school and later worked as a houseboy.

Locke returned to China in 1927 and married Lew Faye-King. He taught English at a Toisan technical school. He later worked in radio communications in Hong Kong. When war with Japan began in 1939, Locke and his eldest son, Paul, came to Seattle. His wife took the other sons, Raymond and Melvin, back to Toisan.

In Seattle, Locke operated the China Star Café on Yesler Way. When World War II broke out, he was rejected for military service but was able to secure a job at the Bremerton shipyard. His wife died in China in 1944. He then married, by "proxy," Louie Mee Siem, who cared for his two orphaned sons.

After the war, Locke returned to work at the China Star Café, and in 1951, his proxy wife and two sons arrived from Toisan. He later purchased and ran, in succession, the Boulder Café, Athenian at the Pike Place Market, and the Lotus Delicatessen near 14th and South Jackson Street.

Meanwhile, the immigrant bachelor society in Chinatown slowly declined. While some returned to China or moved elsewhere, others still harbored hopes of returning to their home villages. Those hopes ended with China's Communist revolution in 1949. The era of the Chinese sojourners was officially over.

With the migration of Chinese families to other neighborhoods, the buildings in the Chinatown core and the surrounding area had become run-down. Behind such successful restaurants at Tai Tung, Hong Kong, Don Ting and Linyen was a rapidly declining Chinatown. The hotel and association buildings showed the wear of age and deferred maintenance. Residents lived in small, substandard rooms with no heat, inadequate plumbing, chipped paint and rodents.

In the late 1940s, the Jackson Street Community Council, a multi-racial self-help group, was formed to improve the declining social and economic conditions and create racial harmony between the Chinese, Japanese, Filipino, African American and white residents in the Chinatown area. The organization brought together business persons and leaders from the different ethnic groups. Ben Woo, James Mar and Anne Chinn Wing were among the Chinese on the Council.

The Jackson Street Community Council was the first organization not exclusively Chinese to become involved with the affairs of Chinatown. Because Chinatown and the immediate surrounding area was multi-racial, the Council referred to the neighborhood as the "International Area." The term "International District," which includes Chinatown, originates from this.

The Jackson Street Community Council was probably the first neighborhood improvement organization in the city. It received national recognition for its achievements. Without the benefit of government funds, the Council managed to clear vacant lots, plant trees on the hillside below Yesler Terrace and sponsor community events to promote the area. One of its most notable achievements was getting the state legislature to allow urban renewal programs. The Council also helped convince the city to pass a housing code ordinance so that absentee property owners would fix up their properties.

The Council, however, was unsuccessful in arguing against the construction of the Interstate 5 freeway through the area. The freeway, the Council argued, would cut Chinatown in half. In 1962, when the freeway was built, the fears of the Council became a reality: the section of Chinatown east of the freeway became an isolated island.

Tennis champion Amy Yee, circa 1950s-1960s. (Courtesy of The Seattle Times)

Like other first generation small business owners, Joe Locke had to work hard to support his family. Four more children were born, bringing the total to seven. Yet, remarkably, he found the energy to play a leadership role in the community. He was active in the Locke Association, Hip Sing Tong and Chong Wa Benevolent Association. He was president of each group for some period of time for nearly three decades beginning in the 1950s.

Many first generation women, if they didn't work in the family business, were employed in the garment or laundry business. Black Manufacturing on Rainier Avenue was one of the larger employers of Chinese garment workers as well as Roffe's, Sportcasters and Pacific Trail. Star Laundry on 12th Avenue between Yesler Way and Fir Street employed a large number of Chinese women. Ability to speak English was not a requirement for employment at these workplaces.

By this time, a frustrated group of young Chinese American professionals started the Chinese Community Service Organization (CCSO). They tried unsuccessfully to convince the Chong Wa Benevolent Association, the representative body for Chinese Americans in Chinatown, to become more active in community improvement projects. But Chong Wa was controlled by elderly men who clung to the "old Chinese way of thinking and doing things." The difference between the two groups was a sign of generational conflict. Both groups wanted the best for the community, but had two ways of going about it. One approach was more Chinese, the other was more American.

On July 6, 1960, Robert Chinn, a grandson of Chinn We-Shing, opened the first Chinese American bank in the state, United Savings and Loan. It was a monumental achievement. While there have been other Chinese American banking institutions in the U.S., United Savings and Loan is one of the few, if not the only one, that survived. It was not easy. At times, Chinn worked without a salary for long hours and, along with the institution's officers, did the janitorial work.

In 1962, 102 years after the first Chinese arrived in Seattle, Wing Luke, whose grandfather was present at the time of the 1886 anti-Chinese riot, was elected to the Seattle City Council.

Luke's parents operated a hand laundry, then a small grocery store, on First Hill. He served as student body president in his senior year at Roosevelt High School. After serving in World War II, he attended the University of Washington, where he was president of the UW Young Democrats and received a law degree. After graduation, he was elected president of the King County Young Democrats and state national committeeman. After working for several years as an assistant attorney general for the state, he took a leave of absence and filed for an open seat on the City Council. Overcoming an anonymous smear campaign, Luke won the primary and general elections and was sworn into office on March 13, 1962. It was a monumental event for the entire Chinese community. Luke became the first Chinese American elected to office in a large American city on the mainland.

As a Council member, Luke fought hard for civil rights and open housing. Returning from a fishing trip in eastern Washington, Luke and two others were killed in a plane crash in 1965. Luke's tragic and untimely death ended the promising career of the rising political star. A public school and a museum in Seattle were named in his honor.

Current and future leaders of the Chinese community in Seattle meet in Ruby Chow's restaurant in 1962. From left: Guay Lee, Warren Chan, Wing Luke, Liem Tuai, Ping Chow, Mabel Yuen, Ruby Chow and George Yee. (Courtesy of Guay Lee)

The Civil Rights Movement swept the country and played a large part in the passage of the 1965 Immigration and Nationality Act. Under this act, a limit of 170,000 immigrants from the eastern hemisphere were allowed to enter the United States annually with a ceiling of 20,000 from each country. Prior to this law, the quota for Chinese was only 105 and it didn't matter which country a Chinese came from. Prior to the 1965 law, Chinese were the only group whose quota was based on national origin.

The changes in immigration law led to the arrival of Chinese from the People's Republic of China, Hong Kong, Taiwan and Southeast Asian countries. In contrast to the early impoverished peasants from the villages, many of these new immigrants were educated, came with money and had been merchants in their homeland. They arrived at a time of seemingly infinite opportunities made possible by the struggles and hardships of the simple country folks from the villages of Toisan, who began paving the road to Seattle 100 years earlier.

Bibliography

Anderson, Gudrun. "Three Generations of Chinese Family which Figures in Queer Story of Wealth and Oriental Tradition." *Seattle Post-Intelligencer*, September 23, 1917.

Bagley, Clarence. *History of King County, Washington*, v. 1. Chicago: Clark Publishing Company, 1927.

de Barros, Paul. *Jackson Street After Hours: The Roots of Jazz in Seattle*. Seattle: Sasquatch Books, 1993.

Bucklock, James. "Seattle's Chinese in Public and Private Life." *Seattle Post-Intelligencer*, October 15, 1912.

"By and By, No More Chinese." *Seattle Post-Intelligencer*, December 13, 1899.

Chan, Sucheng. *Asian Americans: An Interpretive History*. Boston: Twayne Publishers, 1991.

Chen, Jack. *The Chinese of America*. San Francisco: Harper and Row, 1980.

Chin, Art. *Golden Tassels: A History of the Chinese in Washington, 1857-1977*. Seattle: Art Chin, 1987.

Chin, Doug and Art. "The Legacy of Washington's Early Chinese Pioneers." *International Examiner*, March 4, 1987.

Chin, Doug and Art. *Uphill: The Settlement and Diffusion of Chinese in Seattle, Washington*. Seattle: Shorey Publications, 1974.

Chin, Doug and Peter Bacho. "The International District: History of an Urban Ethnic Neighborhood in Seattle." *International Examiner*, October 16, 1985.

"Chin Gee Hee, Noted Seattle Chinese, Dead." *The Seattle Times*, July 1, 1929.

"Chinese for Canneries." *Seattle Post-Intelligencer*, April 4, 1900.

"Chinese Start Right." *The Seattle Times*, March 19, 1942.

Chinn, Thomas W. and Phillip Choy. *A History of Chinese in California: A Syllabus*. San Francisco: Chinese American Historical Society, 1969.

Evans, Walter. "Bicentennial Biographies: Wing Luke." *Seattle Post-Intelligencer*, September 12, 1975.

"Faces of the City: Chinatown Hushed, Charlie Louie is Dead." *The Seattle Times*, October 20, 1964.

Friday, Chris G. "Silent Sojourn: The Chinese Along the Lower Columbia, 1870-1900." *Annals of the Chinese Historical Society of the Pacific Northwest*. Bellingham: Chinese Historical Society of the Pacific Northwest, 1985-86.

Guimary, Donald and Jack Masson. "The Exploitation of Chinese Labor in the Alaska Salmon Industry." *Chinese America: History and Perspectives*. San Francisco: Chinese Historical Society of America, 1990.

Hildebrand, Lorraine Barker. *Straw Hats, Sandals and Steel: The Chinese in Washington State*. Tacoma: Washington State American Revolution Bicentennial Commission, 1977.

History of Chinese in Seattle. Exhibit, Wing Luke Memorial Museum. Seattle: November 15, 1975 to February 2, 1976.

Johnson, Dorothy and Charles M. Gates. *Empire of the Columbia: A History of the Pacific Northwest*. New York: Harper and Row, 1957.

Jue, Willard. "Chin Gee Hee, Chinese Pioneer Entrepreneur in Seattle and Toishan." *Annals of the Chinese Historical Society of the Pacific Northwest*. Seattle: Chinese Historical Society of the Pacific Northwest, 1983.

Jue, Willard and Silas. "Goon Dip, Entrepreneur, Diplomat and Community Leader." *Annals of the Chinese Historical Society of the Pacific Northwest*. Bellingham: Chinese Historical Society of the Pacific Northwest, 1984.

Karlin, Jules A. "The Anti-Chinese Outbreaks in Seattle, 1885-1886." *Pacific Northwest Quarterly*, n. 39, 1948.

Kay, Lew G. "Seattle Chinese." *The Coast Magazine*, December, 1909.

Kinnear, George. *Anti-Chinese Riots at Seattle, Washington, February 8, 1886*. Seattle: NP, 1911.

Kreisman, Lawrence. "National Register of Historic Places Inventory – Nomination Form – King Street Historical District." Seattle: Office of Urban Conservation, 1986.

Lee, Rose Hum. *The Chinese in the United States*. Hong Kong: Hong Kong University Press, 1960.

Lyman, Stanford M. *Chinese Americans*. New York: Random House, 1974.

Mark, Diane Mei Lin and Ginger Chih. *A Place Called Chinese America*. Dubuque: Kendall/Hunt Publishing, 1982.

McCunn, Ruthanne Lum. *Chinese American Portraits*. San Francisco: Chronicle Press, 1980.

McDonald, Lucille. "Seattle's First Chinese Resident." *The Seattle Times Magazine*, September 11, 1955.

Morgan, Murray. *Skid Road: An Informal Portrait of Seattle*. New York: Viking Press, 1960.

"Progressive Chinese Men and Firms of Seattle." *Seattle Post-Intelligencer*, April 27, 1902.

Reddin, John. "Faces of the City: Sun Yat-Sen's Visit to Seattle." *The Seattle Times*, February 23, 1972.

Sale, Roger. *Seattle Past to Present*. Seattle: University of Washington Press, 1976.

Scheare, Rillmand. "The Quiet Revolution in Chinatown." *Seattle Magazine*, 1964.

Schmid, Calvin F., Charles E. Nobbe and Arlene E. Mitchell. *Non-white Races, State of Washington*. Olympia: Washington State Planning and Community Affairs Agency, 1968.

Takaki, Ronald. *Strangers from a Different Shore: A History of Asian Americans*. New York: Penguin Books, 1989.

Takami, David. "Shared Dreams: A History of Asians and Pacific Americans in Washington State." Olympia: Washington Centennial Commission, 1989.

Wynne, Robert E. *Reaction to the Chinese in the Pacific Northwest and British Columbia*. New York: Arno Press, 1978.

Index of Individuals in Alphabetical Order with Listing of Immediate Family Relationships within the Book and Interview and Photo Credits

Chan, Violette, mother of Warren Chan..................29
Interview by Jill Chan, October 14, 1990.
Photo courtesy of Chan Family.

Chan, Warren, son of Violette Chan..................168
Interview by Ron Chew, June 17, 1991.
Photo by John D. Pai.

Chew, Gam Har, wife of Gregory H. Chew..................132
Interview by Ron Chew, March 27, 1998.
Photo by John D. Pai.

Chew, Gregory H., husband of Gam Har Chew..................92
Interview by Ron Chew, October 6 and 27, 1990.
Photo by Dean Wong.

Chew, Sen Poy..................126
Interview by Ron Chew, July 24, 1996.
Photo by John D. Pai.

Chin, Bill L...................52
Interview by Ron Chew, January 17, 1991.
Photo by Dean Wong.

Chin, Gim..................131
Interview by Yanlan Yang, c.1990.
Photo by John D. Pai.

Chin, Hen Sen..................114
Interview by Susan Chin, December 30, 1990.
Photo by Dean Wong.

Chin, Henry..................72
Interview by Ron Chew, November 26, 1990.
Photo by Dean Wong.

Chin, Hong Y...................118
Interview by JoAnne Lee and Bertha Tsuchiya, c.1991.
Photo courtesy of Daisy Kwan Chin.

Chin, Myra Mar, sister of James Mar..................49
Interview by Ron Chew and Debbie Louie, January 11, 1991.
Photo by John D. Pai.

Chin, Yu Sung..................130
Interview by Candace Chin, November 24, 1990.
Photo by John D. Pai.

Chinn, Andrew, brother of Nellie Chinn Woo..................73
Interview by Bettie Sing Luke, March 7, 1991.
Photo by John D. Pai.

Chinn, Hing W...................10
Interview by Ron Chew and Susan Kunimatsu, July 29, 1993.
Photo by Dean Wong.

Chinn, Hing Y., husband of Mary Doung Chinn................................86
   Interview by Ron Chew, May 29 and November 29, 1991.
   Interview by Cassie Chinn, July 19, 2002.
   Photo by John D. Pai.
Chinn, Lawrence P., half-brother of Wallace "Pudge" Eng, Winnie Tuai, Rose Chinn Wong...156
   Interview by Greg Tuai, February 12, 1991.
   Photo by Dean Wong.
Chinn, Mary Doung, wife of Hing Y. Chinn.....................................101
   Interview by Ron Chew, May 29, 1991.
   Photo by John D. Pai.
Chinn, Raymond, brother of Florence Eng Chin................................50
   Interview by Ron Chew and Susan Kunimatsu, July 15, 1993.
   Photo by Dean Wong.
Chinn, Ruby Au, sister of Patricia Au Kan..14
   Interview by Cynthia Kan Rekdal, June 20, 1991.
   Photo by Dean Wong.
Chinn, Ruth Jung..174
   Interview by Ron Chew and Debbie Louie, September 29, 1993.
   Photo by Dean Wong.
Chinn, Walter, brother of Wilma C. Woo..20
   Interview by Kathryn Chinn, November 8, 1990.
   Photo by Dean Wong.
Chong, Frank L...116
   Interview by Ron Chew and Ian Chong, January 11, 1991.
   Photo by John D. Pai.
Chow, Ruby..152
   Interview by Ron Chew, February 28, 1994.
   Photo by Dean Wong.
Chu, Roy...22
   Interview by Janine Chu, May 19, 1995.
   Photo by John D. Pai.
Chun, Dorothy, mother-in-law of Ben Woo.......................................120
   Interview by Ron Chew, September 1, 4 and 11, 1992.
   Interview by Ron Chew and John D. Pai, February 10, 1994.
   Interview by Ron Chew, August 16, 1996.
   Photo by Dean Wong.
Dong, Bruce, brother of Vincent Y. Dong..80
   Interview by Juliette Dong Yamane, March 24, 1991.
   Photo by Dean Wong.
Dong, Vincent Y., brother of Bruce Dong..144
   Interview by Selena Dong, December 30, 1990.
   Photo courtesy of Juliette Dong Yamane.

Edwards, Jessie..69
   Interview by Janine Chu, March 9 and 16, 1995.
   Photo by John D. Pai.
Eng, Florence Chin, sister of Raymond Chinn......................................8
   Interview by Ron Chew, November 15, 1990.
   Photo by Dean Wong.
Eng, Wai..122
   Interview by Ron Chew and Kathryn Chinn, May 11, 1991.
   Interview by Ron Chew, October 13, 1993.
   Photo by John D. Pai.
Eng, Wallace "Pudge", brother of Winnie Tuai, Rose Chinn Wong, half-brother of Lawrence P. Chinn...70
   Interview by Ron Chew, September 4, 1996.
   Photo by John D. Pai.
Eng, William..66
   Interview by Serena Louie, October 11, 1990.
   Photo by Dean Wong.
Fung, Calvin, husband of Jeni Kay Fung...172
   Interview by Ron Chew, January 25, 1991.
   Photo by John D. Pai.
Fung, Jeni Kay, wife of Calvin Fung, sister of Henry Kay Lock....102
   Interview by Ron Chew, January 25, 1991.
   Photo by Dean Wong.
Goon, Clifton..45
   Interview by Ron Chew, October 9, 1990.
   Photo by John D. Pai.
Ham, George...140
   Interview by Ron Chew, June 13, 1991.
   Photo by Dean Wong.
Hing, Henry..76
   Interview by Ron Chew and Debbie Louie, October 12, 1995.
   Photo courtesy of Henry Hing.
Ho, Frances Chin..142
   Interview by April Eng, September 16, 1990.
   Photo by April Eng.
Jang, Lohman, husband of Nancy Jang...99
   Interview by Ron Chew, November 2, 1994.
   Photo by John D. Pai.
Jang, Nancy, wife of Lohman Jang..78
   Interview by Ron Chew, November 2, 1994.
   Photo by John D. Pai.
Jue, Gertrude..137
   Interview by Jue Family, September 2001.
   Photo courtesy of Bennett Jue.

Jue, Priscilla Chong, sister of Louise Yook..........................38
  Interview by April Eng, February 28, 1991.
  Interview by Ron Chew, October 15, 1991 and June 4, 1997.
  Photo by John D. Pai.
Kan, Patricia Au, sister of Ruby Au Chinn..........................16
  Interview by Paisley Rekdal, June 20, 1991.
  Interview by Melissa Szeto Matsuda, April 28, 1998.
  Photo by John D. Pai.
Kay, Bill, husband of Toy Kay..........................36
  Interview by Ron Chew, December 7, 1991.
  Photo by John D. Pai.
Kay, Helen Eng, wife of Richard Lew Kay..........................150
  Interview by Bettie Sing Luke, March 25, 1991.
  Photo by John D. Pai.
Kay, Richard Lew, husband of Helen Eng Kay, brother of Marjorie L. Lee..........................112
  Interview by Bettie Sing Luke, March 25, 1991.
  Photo by Dean Wong.
Kay, Toy, wife of Bill Kay..........................136
  Interview by Ron Chew, December 7, 1991.
  Photo by John D. Pai.
Ko, Eugene..........................110
  Interview by Kathryn Chinn, June 15, 1991.
  Photo by John D. Pai.
Lee, Bill..........................108
  Interview by Joyce Eng, June 1998.
  Photo by John D. Pai.
Lee, Gee Min..........................128
  Interview by Ron Chew, July 31, 1996.
  Photo by John D. Pai.
Lee, Guay..........................82
  Interview by JoAnne Lee and Bertha Tsuchiya, November 3, 1990.
  Photo by Dean Wong.
Lee, Marjorie L., sister of Richard Lew Kay..........................46
  Interview by Ron Chew, July 6, 1995.
  Photo by John D. Pai.
Lew, Daniel Hong..........................124
  Interview by Ron Chew, March 3, 1994.
  Photo by John D. Pai.
Lock, Henry Kay, brother of Jeni Kay Fung..........................74
  Interview by Jeni Kay Fung, June 5, 1991.
  Photo courtesy of Jeni Kay Fung.
Locke, Helen Woo, sister of David H. Woo, Henry H. Woo, May G. Woo..........................44
  Interview by Ron Chew, 1992-1994.
  Photo courtesy of Helen Woo Locke.
Locke, James..........................106
  Interview by Ron Chew, February 20, 1998.
  Photo by John D. Pai.
Locke, Loy Hugh..........................34
  Interview by Ron Chew, March 28, 1992.
  Photo by Dean Wong.
Louie, Art..........................146
  Interview by John D. Pai, c.1994.
  Photo by John D. Pai.
Louie, Henry..........................26
  Interview by Ron Chew, December 23, 1996 and January 30, 1997.
  Photo by John D. Pai.
Louie, Henry, brother of Ken Louie..........................160
  Interview by Debbie Louie, September 22, 1993.
  Photo by Dean Wong.
Louie, James..........................64
  Interview by Ron Chew, July 29, 1996.
  Photo by John D. Pai.
Louie, Ken, brother of Henry Louie..........................18
  Interview by Debbie Louie, September 22, 1993.
  Photo by Dean Wong.
Louie, Paul..........................60
  Interview by Ron Chew, May 6, 1992.
  Photo by John D. Pai.
Luke, Keye..........................148
  Interview by Heidi Chang, December 31, 1990.
  Photo courtesy of Ethel Longenecker.
Luke, Steven..........................162
  Interview by Ron Chew, July 24, 1996.
  Photo by John D. Pai.
Lum, Art B...........................154
  Interview by Ron Chew, June 18, 1991.
  Photo by John D. Pai.
Lung, Fannie Eng..........................28
  Interview by Bertha Tsuchiya and Gloria Lung Wakayama, February 2, 1991.
  Photo by Dean Wong.
Mar, Alfred C...........................94
  Interview by Ron Chew and Susan Kunimatsu, August 16, 1993.
  Photo by Dean Wong.

Mar, Chong Wing..98
   Interview by Ron Chew, January 10, 1995.
   Photo by John D. Pai.

Mar, Dan..161
   Interview by Ron Chew, August 15, 1996.
   Interview by Lily Eng, November 10, 1998.
   Photo by John D. Pai.

Mar, James, brother of Myra Mar Chin.................................32
   Interview by Ron Chew and Susan Kunimatsu, August 16 and
   September 23, 1993.
   Photo by Dean Wong.

Mar, Jeni Dong..62
   Interview by Ron Chew, August 22, 1996.
   Photo courtesy of Jeni Dong Mar.

Mar, Ruth..139
   Interview by Ron Chew, July 3, 1992.
   Photo by John D. Pai.

Mark, Tsee Watt..138
   Interview by Ron Chew, July 31, 1996.
   Photo courtesy of Sue Mark.

Moy, Eddie..158
   Interview by Ron Chew, January 5, 1995.
   Photo by Dean Wong.

Tuai, Liem Eng, husband of Winnie Tuai.............................170
   Interview by Ron Chew, October 13, 1990.
   Photo by John D. Pai.

Tuai, Winnie, wife of Liem Eng Tuai, sister of Wallace "Pudge"
Eng, Rose Chinn Wong, half-sister of Lawrence P. Chinn................68
   Interview by Gregory Tuai, August 25, 1996.
   Photo courtesy of Walter Tuai.

Wing, Anne Chinn..40
   Interview by Marcella Wing, May 17, 1991.
   Photo by Dean Wong.

Wong, Allan Fay..173
   Interview by Heidi Chang, December 3, 1990.
   Photo by Dean Wong.

Wong, Fung Sinn..134
   Interview by Maxine Chan, November 24, 1990.
   Interview by Melissa Szeto Matsuda, March 24, 1998.
   Photo by Dean Wong.

Wong, Harry, husband of Rose Chinn Wong.........................12
   Interview by Ron Chew, June 3, 1997.
   Photo by John D. Pai.

Wong, Homer..164
   Interview by Ron Chew, August 8, 1996.
   Photo by John D. Pai.

Wong, James..24
   Interview by Ron Chew, October 19 and 23, 1990.
   Photo by Dean Wong.

Wong, Puey King..135
   Interview by Ron Chew, December 15, 1998.
   Photo by Dean Wong.

Wong, Rose Chinn, wife of Harry Wong, sister of Wallace "Pudge"
Eng, Winnie Tuai, half-sister of Lawrence P. Chinn.........................58
   Interview by Ron Chew, July 16, 1997.
   Photo by John D. Pai.

Wong, Tek..23
   Interview by Ron Chew and Debbie Louie, November 2, 1995.
   Photo courtesy of Wong family.

Woo, Ben, son-in-law of Dorothy Chun.................................84
   Interview by Ron Chew, February 9, 1992.
   Photo by Dean Wong.

Woo, David H., brother of Helen Woo Locke, Henry H. Woo, May
G. Woo...104
   Interview by Ron Chew, October 29 and November 2, 1990 and
   August 1, 1991.
   Photo by Dean Wong.

Woo, Henry H., husband of Josephine Chinn Woo, brother of Helen
Woo Locke, David H. Woo, May G. Woo..............................42
   Interview by Ron Chew, October 10, 1992.
   Interview by Ron Chew and Serena Woo, August 2 and 3, 1996.
   Photo by John D. Pai.

Woo, Josephine Chinn, wife of Henry H. Woo.......................56
   Interview by Ron Chew, May 6, 1992 and August 3, 1996.
   Photo by John D. Pai.

Woo, Mary..96
   Interview by Ron Chew, June 7, 1999.
   Photo by John D. Pai.

Woo, Mary Luke..54
   Interview by Ron Chew, April 8, 1997.
   Photo by John D. Pai.

Woo, May G., sister of Helen Woo Locke, David H. Woo, Henry
H. Woo..100
   Interview by Ron Chew, 1990-1994.
   Photo courtesy of David H. Woo.

Woo, Melvin..88
   Interview by Ron Chew, September 8, 2000.
   Photo by John D. Pai.

Woo, Nellie Chinn, sister of Andrew Chinn..31
  Interview by Jeni Kay Fung, Shannon Gee and John D. Pai, August 26, 1996.
  Photo courtesy of Ginlin Woo.

Woo, Wilma C., sister of Walter Chinn..89
  Interview by Ron Chew, December 9, 1990.
  Photo by Yuen Lui Studios.

Wu, Harriett..48
  Interview by Ron Chew, October 19, 1991.
  Photo by Dean Wong.

Yee, George K...167
  Interview by Yanlan Yang, c.1990.
  Photo courtesy of Fred Yee.

Yee, James..166
  Interview by Ron Chew, August 30, 1996.
  Photo by John D. Pai.

Yee, Sam..90
  Interview by Amy Wong and Fred Yee, May 19, 1991.
  Photo by Dean Wong.

Yook, Louise, sister of Priscilla Chong Jue..30
  Interview by April Eng, May 16, 1991.
  Interview by Melissa Szeto Matsuda, April 2, 1998.
  Photo by John D. Pai.

Young, Lee Hong "Smiley"..129
  Interview by Ron Chew, September 4, 1996.
  Interview by Cassie Chinn, January 7, 1998.
  Photo by John D. Pai.

Acknowledgments

Thanks to all the individuals who generously agreed to be interviewed for the Chinese Oral History Project: Violette Chan, Warren Chan, Gam Har Chew, Gregory H. Chew, Sen Poy Chew, Bill L. Chin, Daisy Kwan Chin, Gim Chin, Hen Sen Chin, Henry Chin, Hong Y. Chin, Myra Mar Chin, Yu Sung Chin, Andrew Chinn, Arlene Chinn, Bob Chinn, Hing W. Chinn, Hing Y. Chinn, Lawrence P. Chinn, Mary Doung Chinn, Raymond Chinn, Ruby Au Chinn, Ruth Jung Chinn, Walter Chinn, Frank L. Chong, Ruby Chow, Roy Chu, Dorothy Chun, Bruce Dong, Vincent Y. Dong, Jessie Edwards, Florence Chin Eng, Jimmie Eng, Wai C. Eng, Wallace "Pudge" Eng, William Eng, Calvin Fung, Jeni Kay Fung, Clifton Goon, George Ham, Henry Hing, Frances Chin Ho, Dorothy Luke Hong, Lohman Jang, Nancy Jang, Gertrude Jue, Priscilla Chong Jue, Patricia Au Kan, Bill Kay, Helen Eng Kay, Richard Lew Kay, Toy Kay, Eugene Ko, Bill Lee, Gee Min Lee, Guay Lee, Marjorie L. Lee, Daniel Hong Lew, Henry Kay Lock, Helen Woo Locke, James Locke, Loy Hugh Locke, Wanda Chin Locke, Art Louie, Henry Louie, Henry Louie, James Louie, Ken Louie, Paul Louie, Keye Luke, Steven Luke, Art B. Lum, Fannie Eng Lung, Alfred C. Mar, Chong Wing Mar, Dan Mar, James Mar, Jeni Dong Mar, Ruth Mar, Tsee Watt Mark, Eddie Moy, Liem Eng Tuai, Winnie Tuai, Anne Chinn Wing, Allan Fay Wong, Fung Sinn Wong, Harry Wong, Homer Wong, James Wong, Puey King Wong, Rose Chinn Wong, Tek Wong, Ben Woo, David H. Woo, Henry H. Woo, Josephine Chinn Woo, Mary Woo, Mary Luke Woo, May G. Woo, Melvin Woo, Nellie Chinn Woo, Wilma C. Woo, Harriett Wu, Amy Yee, George K. Yee, Sam Yee, Louise Yook and Lee Hong "Smiley" Young.

Thanks to the following individuals who conducted and transcribed interviews: Jill Chan, Maxine Chan, Heidi Chang, Ron Chew, Candace Chin, Doug Chin, Grace Chin, Susan Chin, Cassie Chinn, Chris Chinn, Kathryn Chinn, Ruth Jung Chinn, Ian Chong, Janine Chu, Selena Dong, April Eng, Joyce Eng, Lily Eng, Jeni Kay Fung, Shannon Gee, Bennett Jue, Susan Kunimatsu, Jeff Lagonoy, JoAnne Lee, Brian Locke, Debbie Louie, Serena Louie, Bettie Sing Luke, Kristi Woo Matsuda, Melissa Szeto Matsuda, John D. Pai, Cynthia Kan Rekdal, Paisley Rekdal, Jill Chan Rinearson, Bertha Tsuchiya, Gregory Tuai, Gloria Lung Wakayama, Marcella Wing, Amy Wong, Ben-Ling Wong, Dean Wong, Rick Wong, Michael Woo, Serena Woo, Juliette Dong Yamane, Yanlan Yang, Fred Yee and Tina Young.

The following individuals and organizations generously provided photographs, labor and support services: May Sheung Ma Chan, David Chattin-McNichols, Art Chin, Daisy Kwan Chin, Donnie Chin, Steve Chin, Hing W. Chinn, Mary Doung Chinn, Shau-Lee Chow, Dorothy Cordova, Raymond Dong, Ginny Eng, Bob Fisher, Jeni Kay Fung, Henry Hing, Bennett Jue, Silas Jue, Eli Felix Kim, Lynn Lee, Raymond Lew, Helen Woo Locke, Ethel Longenecker, Andy Louie, Ruby Macadangdang, Dan Mar, Jeni Dong Mar, Paul Mar, Sue Mark, Esther Mumford, Museum of History and Industry, Loan Nguyen, *The Seattle Times*, Kamol Sudthayakorn, David Takami, Suelene Tom, Elizabeth Umbanhowar, Walter Tuai, Rita Wang, Rick Wong, Celeste Woo, David H. Woo, Ginlin Woo, Regina M. Woo, Serena Woo, Juliette Dong Yamane and Fred Yee.

Special thanks to project photographers John D. Pai and Dean Wong, and calligraphers Zuo-lie Deng and Reverend Paul Szeto.

This second edition would not have been completed without the financial contributions of organizations and individuals too numerous to comprehensively list. We are grateful to them all.

Prime Sponsor
The Tuai Family

Major Sponsors
The Boeing Company
Bon-Macy*s

Sponsors
American Legion Cathay Post #186
Jeni and Cal Fung
Faye and Janie Hong
Helen and Richard Kay
Paul Mar
Marpac Construction
Dean and Gloria Lung Wakayama

Supporters
Linda Chew and Roy Burt
Ark and Winnie Chin
Daisy K. Chin
Raymond and Ling Chinn
Janine Chu and Daniel Bernstein
Chris Galloway and Rebecca Brown
Alicia Davis
Hong's Garden
Vera and Joey Ing
Jade Guild
Nancy Jang
Helen and Calvin Lang
Calvin and Ruth Locke
James and Julie Locke
James and Ida Mar
Gene and Priscilla Moy
Isaac and Lensey Namioka
Mary L. Pang
Connie So and Brett Eckelberg
Nelson and Yolande Wong
Josephine Woo
Nellie Chinn Woo